Praise for
The Speaker's Coach

'There is no single set formula to giving a great talk. However, in this book you will find compelling insights and practical guidance to help you discover the way that's right for you.'

Chris Anderson, Head, TED

'Bursting with anecdotes, tips and techniques. This book is an essential guide for anyone who wants to improve their presentation skills.'

Jason Yeomanson, Leadership and Management Development Consultant, Marks & Spencer

'These sixty secrets make such sense. They are simple and easily enacted. After reading this, you will be unable to make a bad speech ever again.'

Neil Mullarkey, co-founder, London's Comedy Store Players; communication expert

'*The Speaker's Coach* is a comprehensive, invaluable and entertaining resource which should be required reading for anyone intending to deliver a presentation. It covers every aspect of the process to ensure phenomenal results.'

Jerome Kaplan MA/CCC-SLP, Speech-Language Pathologist, Boston University Aphasia Resource Centre

'Graham Shaw is a renowned public speaker and this book distills some of his expertise into highly practical tips that make a real difference. His trade secrets are illustrated in his own inimitable style, making this both a useful and entertaining read. Have no doubt, whether you are new at public speaking or a seasoned veteran, you are sure to find some great tips inside that will transform the delivery and value of your presentations.'

John Swallow, Head of Learning and Development, Specsavers Northern Europe

'If you are being asked to deliver presentations either at work or elsewhere, this book is for you. Graham's super 60 tips will enable you to feel even more confident, competent and relaxed in front of your audience and deliver your message with great impact.'

David Haskell, Learning and Development Manager, Greater Anglia

'Graham continues to create engaging and entertaining resources to help anyone through the potentially daunting prospect of presenting. Whether you're new to presenting or need help in a particular area, this book will be your go-to. An absolute recommended read.'

Denise Tillson, Learning and Development Specialist, Holiday Extras

'I love simple 'how to' books. *The Speaker's Coach* is an easy read - content-packed, bullet-point driven, and a must for anyone wanting to be a better presenter.'

Michael Heppell, professional speaker; author, *How to Be Brilliant*

'This book will help turn your presentation into a masterpiece! *The Speaker's Coach* is a true gem; an engaging guide providing you with all the tools you need in order to really "wow" your audience and boost your confidence in public speaking. Learn lots of tips and tricks including: why the pace of your voice makes a difference, how to remember the names of your audience (and make your delivery extra-personal) and how to really make a positive impact on your audience. Reading this book will help overcome a few fears whilst presenting and increase your ability to build effective talks and workshops that help the audience to take away something meaningful.'

Naeema Pasha, Director of Henley Careers, Henley Business School, University of Reading

'This book unlocks the secrets of how to become and amazing public speaker. It is a game-changer.'

Laura Bodwick, personal development coach

'I found it to be an accessible, practical and compelling resource for all who may ever have an audience. It walks the reader through key steps and strategies to ensure that a speaker's personality and character shine through to the listener. The author's use of common sense and humour makes the task seem almost manageable. A must have for novice and experienced speakers alike!'

Dr Elizabeth Hoover, CCC-SLP, BC-ANCDS, Clinical Associate Professor, SLHS, Boston University

'Graham Shaw has written a must-read primer for anyone looking to sharpen their public speaking. This book is full of practical ways to galvanize your inner TED speaker.'

Vlad Gozman, Founder and Curator, TEDxVienna

The Speaker's Coach

Pearson

At Pearson, we have a simple mission: to help people make more of their lives through learning.

We combine innovative learning technology with trusted content and educational expertise to provide engaging and effective learning experiences that serve people wherever and whenever they are learning.

From classroom to boardroom, our curriculum materials, digital learning tools and testing programmes help to educate millions of people worldwide – more than any other private enterprise.

Every day our work helps learning flourish, and wherever learning flourishes, so do people.

To learn more, please visit us at **www.pearson.com/uk**

The Speaker's Coach

60 secrets to make your talk, speech or presentation amazing

Graham Shaw

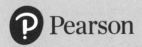 Pearson

Harlow, England • London • New York • Boston • San Francisco • Toronto • Sydney
Dubai • Singapore • Hong Kong • Tokyo • Seoul • Taipei • New Delhi
Cape Town • São Paulo • Mexico City • Madrid • Amsterdam • Munich • Paris • Milan

PEARSON EDUCATION LIMITED

KAO Two
KAO Park
Harlow CM17 9NA
United Kingdom
Tel: +44 (0)1279 623623
Web: www.pearson.com/uk

First edition published 2019 (print and electronic)

ISBN: 978-1-292-25094-6 (print)
      978-1-292-25095-3 (PDF)
      978-1-292-25096-0 (ePub)

British Library Cataloguing-in-Publication Data
A catalogue record for the print edition is available from the British Library

Library of Congress Cataloging-in-Publication Data
A catalog record for the print edition is available from the Library of Congress

10 9 8 7 6 5 4 3 2 1
23 22 21 20 19

Cover design by Madras
Print edition typeset in 9/13pt Helvetica Neue LT W1G by Pearson CSC
Printed by Ashford Colour Press Ltd, Gosport
NOTE THAT ANY PAGE CROSS REFERENCES REFER TO THE PRINT EDITION

Contents

About the author

Graham is an international speaker, speaker coach and specialist in the art of communication. Working worldwide with numerous major organisations, he has helped countless people learn how to give great talks, speeches and presentations. He has coached many TEDx speakers to prepare and deliver their talks to large audiences with confidence and impact.

Graham's talks at TEDxHull and TEDxVienna been viewed by millions online and can be seen on the TED website video library of talks.

He is also the author of 'The Art of Business Communication', which was shortlisted for the 'Management Book of the Year 2016' by the Chartered Management Institute. The book shows the reader how anyone can draw simple sketches to present ideas in memorable ways.

Graham lives near London and is a keen runner with a love of art, psychology and sport.

To learn more about Graham's work, visit www.visionlearning.co.uk

Graham is a regular speaker on the art of communication at conferences and in-house events. To enquire about booking him for your organisation contact info@visionlearning.co.uk and www.visionlearning.co.uk

Acknowledgements

Firstly I owe a huge thank you to Eloise Cook at Pearson Education. Your perceptive insights and feedback throughout the writing process helped me so much. Thank you also to the whole Pearson team and in particular Felicity Baines, Melanie Carter, Dr Priyadharshini Dhanagopal and Sarah Owens for your brilliant work.

A massive thank you goes to my amazingly supportive and patient wife Lynda. I don't know how you put up with me with testing numerous ideas, drafts and cartoon gags on you, but I do appreciate it.

Thank you Ann McCullogh, my ultra-efficient assistant, for all you do, and especially for applying your linguistic expertise to check the manuscript. Likewise, thank you to my great friend Martin Austin for your constructive feedback on my drafts and your fantastic help throughout.

A special thank you is due to my long-time friend and former fellow-trainer Jan Jewers. The generous support you have given to my work as a speaker and author has been invaluable.

Many other people have helped shape my thinking through mentoring, coaching, promoting my work or giving of their time. I thank you all and especially Bernard Amos, Kimberley Hare, the late-Patrick Hare, Nigel and Jenny Heath, Henrietta Lait, Chris McCloskey, Neil Mullarkey, Louise Robb, Pamela Lupton-Bowers, Penny Tompkins and James Lawley, Julian Russell, David and Elizabeth Soehren, Ed Thomas and Rod Webb.

I have had brilliant teachers in the field of Neuro-Linguistic Programming (NLP). Thank you in particular Sue Knight, Ian Ross, John Overdurf and Julie Silverthorn. You have all made such a difference.

Fellow-trainers and speakers have been a source of great support and taught me so much. I am grateful to you all, especially Jan Boyd, Tim Fearon, Nic Hallett, Liz Howell, Sue Harley, Rob Hayes, Cricket Kemp, Will Lakeman, Alastair Olby, Graham Smith, and Neil Tappenden.

Thank you also to my many audiences and workshop participants including teachers, students and children. You have all played a part in helping me to shape my thinking. Likewise I thank my clients for their encouragement over the years, in particular Maria Conte and John Swallow.

There are numerous authors, speakers and researchers on whose work I have drawn, including many TED and TEDx speakers.

I am so grateful to Helen Bissett and the TEDxHull team and also Vlad Gozman Founder of TEDx Vienna and his team for giving me those opportunities to speak from which I learnt so much.

To my sons David and Andrew and daughter-in-law Katy, thank you for your constant support. Thank you also to my parents, Mary and the late-Bill Shaw, for all your encouragement and everything you have done for me.

Finally, I dedicate this book to my delightful grandson, one year-old Finley Shaw, who doesn't need a book on how to captivate an audience.

Publisher's acknowledgements

4 **Abraham Lincoln:** Quote by Abraham Lincoln 5 **Hachette UK:** Chris Anderson, TED Talks - the Official TED Guide to Public Speaking, 11 **CompletelyNovel:** Gavin Miekle, The Presenter's Edge, CompletelyNovel. 16 **Benjamin Franklin:** Quote by Benjamin Franklin 22 **Yogi Berra:** Quote by Yogi Berra 44 **HarperCollins:** Joseph O'Connor and John Seymour, 'Introducing NLP' 45 **Pearson Education:** 'The Leader's Guide to Presenting' by Tom Bird and Jeremy Cassell 48 **John Wiley & Sons:** 'Resonate – present visual stories that transform audiences' by Nancy Duarte 49 **Author's Choice Publishing,:** Words That Change Minds, Shelley Rose Charvet 62 **HarperCollins:** Hare Brain Tortoise Mind, Guy Claxton 65 **Pearson Education:** Garr Reynolds, Presentation Zen 77 **Taylor & Francis:** Lionel Standing 'Learning 10 000 Pictures' - Quarterly Journal of Experimental Psychology 83 **CompletelyNovel:** Gavin

Miekle, The Presenter's Edge, CompletelyNovel. **97 TED Conferences, LLC:** David Epstein's talk at TED2014 **97 TED Conferences, LLC:** Susan Pinkner at TED2017 **100 Macmillan Publishers:** Carmine Gallo, Talk Like TED **103 Developing Company Press:** James Lawley and Penny Tomkins, Metaphors in Mind **103 Crown House Publishing Ltd:** Wendy Sullivan and Judy Rees, Clean Language **103 L. Smithers Publishers:** Oscar Wilde, The Importance of Being Earnest, L. Smithers, 1899. **105 Random House:** Made to Stick, Chip and Dan Heath **114 TED Conferences, LLC:** Amy Cuddy – speaking at TED about research at Harvard University **115 Hachette UK:** Sue Knight, NLP at Work **118 On-Demand Publishing, LLC:** Wendy Palmer and Janet Crawford, Leadership Embodiment **118 Amanda Carlson:** Amanda Carlson Performance Nutritionist **122 Hachette UK:** Chris Anderson, quotes Mary Roach in TED Talks **128 Hachette UK:** Chris Anderson, mentions Clay Shirky in 'TED Talks' **130 Jamey Aebersold Jazz:** Kenny Werner, Effortless Mastery **131 Bill Gates:** Quote by Bill Gates **132 Hachette UK:** Chris Anderson, Quotes Rachel Botsman in TED Talks **133 Hachette UK:** Quoted Rachel Botsman, Oxford University lecturer, author and TED speaker in 'TED Talks' by Chris Anderson **139 Pearson Education:** Emma Ledden, The Presentation Book **142 David Oppenheimer:** Quote by David Oppenheimer **143 David Oppenheimer:** Quote by David Oppenheimer **144 Adam Frankel:** Adam Frankel was Speechwriter to Barack Obama **144 Adam Frankel:** Adam Frankel Speech Writer to Barack Obama **147 Matthias Gruber:** Co-author of the study, Matthias Gruber **148 TED Conferences, LLC:** Robert Waldinger TEDx Beacon Street 2015 **150 Elsevier Inc:** Douglas L. Hintzman on his laboratory research 'Psychology of Learning and Motivation' Vol. 10 1976 **151 Jane D'Arcy:** Jane D'Arcy, Executive Speech Coach **151 Winston Churchill:** Quote by Winston Churchill **152 Jane D'Arcy:** Jane D'Arcy, Executive Speech Coach **152 Bill Gates:** TED talks, Bill Gates **161 Hachette UK:** Simon Raybould, Presentation Genius. **161 Hachette UK:** Chris Anderson, TED Talks, Hachette UK **163 John Cawthorn:** Shakespeare's Hamlet **180 Pearson Education:** Amanda Vickers, Steve Bavister and Jackie Smith, Personal Impact **184 John Wiley & Sons:** Graham Davies, The Presentation Coach **186 Olivia Mitchell:** Olivia Mitchell – Speaking Coach **194 CompletelyNovel:** Gavin Miekle, The Presenter's Edge, CompletelyNovel. **215 Pear Press:** John Medina, Brain Rules **215 SAGE Publications:** Eric Jensen, Brain-Based Learning **238 Hachette UK:** Chris Anderson, TED Talks, Hachette UK

Introduction

When you see an outstanding performance in a talk, speech or presentation, the speaker makes it look easy. However, it does not just happen by magic and is the result of thorough preparation and practice. It is a myth that 'you can either do it or you cannot' and the fact is that these skills can be learnt. However, much of what a great speaker does to be successful is not obvious to the audience, and nor should it be. The techniques of presenting should be invisible to the audience because they are absorbed in the content.

A browse through this book could be a good place!

Cartoon illustrations by Graham Shaw

The purpose of this book is to take you behind the scenes and share with you the secrets of an amazing talk, speech or presentation. I will be your speaker coach and help you to learn exactly how you too can keep audiences on the edge of their seats. Whether you are new to public speaking or already experienced, the secrets in this book will help you develop your ability to engage audiences.

Why invest time in learning public speaking skills?

Think beyond the talk, speech or presentation to the results you want to achieve.

A well-delivered talk can help you to:

- make a difference;
- cause people to think in new ways;
- motivate your audience to take action to support a cause;
- pitch an idea;
- further your career;
- inspire a team to perform well;
- make a positive difference to a social occasion;
- and so much more.

When you speak with confidence in public, there is no end to the potential benefits for yourself and your audience.

Why should you listen to me?

I wrote this book because I love helping people to enhance their public speaking skills. In the relatively short time it will take you to read this book, you will learn the very best ideas that I have gleaned in over 20 years working internationally as a professional speaker and speaker coach.

I have spoken at TEDx events, conferences, seminars and training sessions. My speaker coaching has included TEDx speakers, business leaders and teams in global organisations. Working with children and teachers in schools, and students and lecturers in universities, has also been helpful in developing my understanding of how to engage groups.

You will also benefit from what I have discovered by researching the art and science of speaking. Finally, I have been fortunate to have been taught speaking skills by many excellent speakers and trainers over the years, so you will gain from their wisdom, too.

What will you learn?

What you have in this book is a wealth of information, ideas and techniques that will help you to develop your public speaking skills, whatever the situation.

The 60 Secrets are logically organised into three parts:

- 1: Preparing;
- 2: Practising;
- 3: Performing.

The consistent format of each Secret will become familiar to you and make it easy to get the learning you need from each one.

You will also find many useful references to books, videos and research. Equally, I refer to TED and TEDx talks because there is so much to learn from them, too.

How to get the best out of this book

There is not one approach to public speaking and, in fact, there are many ways that work equally well. Every speaker is different and every talk is different. Therefore, as you read through the book, choose those ideas and techniques that you feel will work best for you and for the kind of talk, speech or presentation you are giving.

How you read the book depends on how you like to learn. Some readers may prefer to read through it from start to finish. However, it works equally well if you dip in and out of it.

This is a practical book with opportunities to apply the skills to your own speaking situations. Each Secret has a *Your turn* activity to help you to develop your knowledge and skills further. Many activities ask you to apply the skills to a talk, speech or presentation of your own. Therefore, you might want to have an example in mind that you can use.

The *Resource for further learning* included in each Secret gives references to books and video clips that help you learn in more depth about that Secret or a related aspect.

So let's get started

To complete the activities, it might be useful to have a pen and paper to hand, along with internet access to be able to watch the recommended videos.

I am delighted to support you in developing your public speaking skills and hope you enjoy this book. Who knows what impact your talks, speeches or presentations could have. Just one of your talks could be the difference that makes the difference for someone – and that could include you.

Part 1

Preparing

1

Think of it this way

Secret 1: If you want to give an amazing talk, pay attention to the details

You cannot absolutely guarantee that a talk, speech or presentation will be amazing because there is no magic wand. But, if you pay enough attention to the details in your preparation, practice and performance, then there is every chance that yours will be.

Why it matters

Attention to detail matters because:

- you will discover those details that make the difference – and those that do not;
- it is unlikely that you will miss out something vital;
- every aspect of your talk will be as good as you can make it;
- knowing how well you are prepared helps you feel comfortable with your talk;
- having confidence in your talk means you are much more likely to perform well on the day;
- the effect of your talk will be more compelling.

It is, of course, still possible to make a mistake. A golfer can win a major tournament yet still hit a few poor shots. Professional musicians often perform in a way that seems faultless to the audience, yet will admit they made a mistake or two. The point is *they are so well prepared* that they have vastly

Practise, practise, practise . . . in front of anyone who will listen

reduced the chances of that happening. As a result, despite an occasional error, their performance is still outstanding. So it is with public speaking.

Everything counts if you want your talk to be amazing.

What to do

1 Prepare well

An amazing talk is the result of an amazing amount of preparation.

Give me six hours to chop down a tree and I will spend the first four sharpening the axe.

Abraham Lincoln

Think ahead and plan carefully. However with so many aspects involved it's not easy to know where to start. The other Secrets in this 'Preparation' section of this book will guide you on *what* to prepare and *how* to do it.

2 Practise thoroughly

Successful speakers leave nothing to chance and it is through repeated practice that they make everything look so natural.

Chris Anderson, Head of TED, refers to 'one of the greatest corporate communicators of recent times', Steve Jobs: 'He put in hours of meticulous rehearsal for every major product launch Apple did. He obsessed over every detail.' Getting the details right in practice will make all the difference to your talk on the day.

See the Secrets in Part 2 Practising to help you to be ready for your talk.

3 Perform confidently

If you have *prepared well* and *practised thoroughly,* then you have a great chance of *performing confidently* on the day. That confident performance, borne out of good planning and practice, is the key to making your talk amazing for the audience.

See Part 3 Performing for guidance on delivering your talk well.

TIP

To create an amazing talk, start preparing sooner than you might think – it takes time.

Your turn

Think back to previous talks, speeches or presentations. Remember how you prepared, practised and performed. For each of those three stages ask:

1 What did you do well?

2 What would you do differently next time?

Keep your notes as a reminder for when you plan your next talk.

Resource for further learning

TED Talks: The Official TED Guide to Public Speaking (2016) by Chris Anderson, Head of TED.

Expert guidance to help you help prepare, practise and perform well.

Secret 2: Help the audience and they will help you

Often, speakers are in fear of the audience and it can feel like a 'you versus them' scenario. However, when you have a helpful mindset, it can positively influence people to support you.

Why it matters

When you think beyond the presentation, often you want the audience to do something as a result. Your outcome is achieved *through them* and, therefore, you need to work *with* them.

Robert Cialdini's research into influence discovered that *reciprocity* is a key factor; people have a natural wish to give something back.

When you adopt a 'helping' mindset it:

- causes you to act in accordance with that positive attitude;
- makes it more likely that the audience will react in a similar way;
- reduces fear, which is an inhibitor of good performance;
- creates a positive atmosphere;
- gets you into a positive state for speaking;
- enables you to flow;
- enhances the desire of people to give their support to your cause.

What to do

1 Give them a compelling outcome

Let people know at the start what's in it for them. Use the ideas in this book about starting well and getting them on your side. Don't be tempted to dive into your topic too quickly before you have done that.

Ken was all set up and confident he could handle the usual trouble-makers

People don't object when you are helping them.

2 Look after their interests

Show the audience you care. You may never have met them before, but that does not mean you cannot care about their interests. See things from their point of view and make sure your content is focused on the benefits for them.

TIP

Focus on what is in it for them.

---

3 Get on well with them

Cialdini's research also found that 'liking' is a key factor in influence. When people like you, usually they will help you more. This is not about being over-friendly, but about building rapport in many different ways. The audience may come to like you through your credibility and authority as much as through a friendly disposition.

4 Give them a great experience

Think of your talk as going on a fascinating journey together with your audience. It is like being the leader on a day out where you want people to have the best time they can. Just as in life, experiences can be serious or light, yet both can be equally important and valuable.

5 Give them your gems of wisdom

Naturally, people might want to be cautious regarding giving away ideas. However, my own experience is not to hold back. When you give people the best information and ideas you possibly can, not only do they benefit, but, ultimately, you will too.

6 Make them the stars

It's natural to think of the speaker as being the star of the show, just like a singer on stage. However, from the perspective of the speaker, it helps if you focus on the audience as the stars. You are giving the talk, but they are the ones who will do something with it. The talk alone is of no use at all. It is only through them that any good is coming of it. They will absorb your ideas and apply them in their own unique ways. Therefore, in that sense, they really are the stars of your talk and it pays to acknowledge that in the way you treat them.

Whatever you speak about, help the audience as much as you can.

Your turn

Bring to mind an upcoming talk. Write down three great reasons why the audience should listen. Make sure to include the biggest benefits to them. Incorporate these in your introduction.

Resource for further learning

Influence: The Psychology of Persuasion (2009) by Robert B. Cialdini.

See also: 'Science of Persuasion' (11-minute video on YouTube) narrated by Robert Cialdini and Steve Martin.

Secret 3: Be yourself, but learn from others to be amazing

If you hear a top sports player or musician being interviewed about how they came to be so excellent in their performances, often they attribute it to others from whom they have learnt. Yet, they still have their own unique style and the same applies to speaking.

Why it matters

Learning from those who are already masters will help you to perform at the top of your 'speaking game'.

- Even if you are a 'natural' speaker, you can always learn.
- *Just* being yourself may feel fine to you – but it may not come across well to others.
- Equally, if you *just* try to be like someone else, you will not be your authentic self.
- Others have taken years to find what works – save time by using their wisdom.
- Everything counts; even small tips can make a big difference.

What to do

1   Learn from other speakers

Next time you see a good speaker, instead of just following the *content* of their talk, focus on their *speaking skills.* Find one speaker online that you really like, e.g. in a TED talk. Observe them carefully and notice what works well. Write down anything they do or say that you could adopt to enhance your own presenting skills.

Monday briefings were never quite the same since Daphne went on that speaking course

2 Learn from related disciplines

There are disciplines with similar skills to those used in giving talks, such as radio and television presenting, comedy or other forms of light entertainment. Watch and listen to *what* they do and *how* they do it. Look for ideas that you could use or adapt.

3 Learn from totally different disciplines

Although it might not seem obvious, there are aspects of high performance in any discipline that you could apply to speaking. For example, an outstanding athlete or musician can teach us a lot. You might see them in action or hear them speak about what they do. You may learn about how they get themselves into a high-performance state or how they recover from an error.

4 Learn from something else you do

There is no doubt that something you are really good at has nothing to do with speaking, such as cooking, gardening, music or sport. Yet, when you think about it, each of those activities will have qualities and skills that can transfer to speaking. These may be being disciplined with your time or preparing well. Bring to mind something that you do well and identify the positive qualities and skills you use that you can transfer to speaking.

5   Learn more about your unique style

Every time you speak is an opportunity to learn more about your own style. Notice what works well and where you can improve. Take time to reflect on your performance and become more self-aware. Ask others for their feedback. Gradually, you will discover what it is about your way of presenting that works. This will enable you to do more of what you do well and stop doing things that are not serving you.

Anyone can be a good speaker. The key is to find your own authentic style.

Gavin Meikle, author of *The Presenter's Edge: How to Unlock Your Inner Speaker*

TIP

Write the one thing you believe you do best as a speaker – and do more of it.

Your turn

1   Think of someone who speaks well – it may be someone you know or not.

2   Write down one thing they do really well.

3   Ask yourself if this is something appropriate to incorporate into your own style.

4   Write down your next chance to incorporate that skill or quality in your own style.

Resource for further learning

'The Speech That Made Obama President', YouTube (six-minute video clip).

Secret 4: Have a conversation rather than give a presentation

A presentation may seem one-way; however, it never really is. The audience are always responding in some way. They communicate through body language such as eye contact, expressions and gestures. They may laugh, cheer or gasp in amazement.

Many are tired of stuffy, formal presentations and it is like a breath of fresh air when a speaker just talks to them in a 'normal' way. It feels much better when a speaker talks *to* an audience rather than *at* them.

Why it matters

Conversations *feel* different from presentations because:

- presentations can have a formal atmosphere;
- conversations often are friendly and informal;
- a conversational style can relax the audience;
- rapport can be built easily with a conversational style.

What to do

Five ways to be more conversational:

1 Think of it *as if* it is a conversation – and you will act *as if* it is

The way you think affects how you come across and changes how the audience responds. That is the power of the mind. When you speak like it is a conversation, they feel as if you are relating to them more personally. Therefore, instead of being in a 'presenting' mindset, think *as if* it is a conversation.

2 Regard the audiences *as if* they are friends you have never met

I used to be apprehensive at the start of any training courses I was leading.

Although the staff loved Jeff, they felt his style could be a little too conversational

I would wonder if some people would be difficult for me to manage. However, when I got to know the course participants, almost everyone always turned out to be very nice.

Then something dawned on me. Instead of waiting to find out, perhaps I could decide from the beginning that they were all nice people. Therefore, I thought of them *as if* they were friends I had never met. It made a huge difference to my confidence.

So think of your audience *as if* they are friends. It will positively change how you perceive them and also how they respond: a 'win-win'.

3 Think of your presentation *as if* it is a story

Presentations can seem like an ordeal to be got through for both presenter and audience. The set of slides can seem like a set of hurdles. However, in a way, a presentation really is a story; it has a beginning, middle and end.

When you think of your presentation as a story, you will explain it better and people will absorb your message more easily. Use the secrets in this book to create a story that keeps people captivated like a book they cannot put down.

TIP

Use the 'as-if' principle to help you achieve what you want in your talks.

---

4 Prepare good links to make it flow easily

A good conversation flows along and a presentation should do the same. The way to achieve this is to make sure you have good links between one point and the next. These links act as signposts and keep people aware of how it all fits together. People like strong links because they can follow you more easily.

5 Do not read – just talk to the audience

Do not read from a script or the slides, unless you need to quote something verbatim. Reading your presentation can make it seem stilted. People can see that you are reading, so it will come across as the opposite of conversational.

Start adopting a conversational style and your audience will enjoy your talks.

Your turn

1 Watch Robert Waldinger's TEDx talk, mentioned below; an excellent example of a conversational style.

2 Write down one thing that he did well that you could emulate.

Resource for further learning

'What makes a good life? Lessons from the longest study on happiness' by Robert Waldinger, TEDxBeaconStreet (12-minute video), www.ted.com

Secret 5: Why 'winging it' is usually a bad idea

'Winging it' can mean giving a talk having not prepared at all or 'flying by the seat of your pants'. But, if a talk is important, then it merits appropriate preparation time and success is seldom achieved without it.

Why it matters

People may 'wing it' because they say they are more relaxed, natural and spontaneous. However, there is no guarantee that such spontaneity will be effective.

In any field of endeavour, great results are rarely achieved in this way. When you see a musician or an athlete perform well, they make it look easy. This is the result of careful preparation and the same rule applies to speaking in public.

Winging it may result in:

● inattention to details that may be critical;

● not anticipating or preparing for objections;

● being caught out by problems that should have been foreseen;

● lack of structure;

● having to think on your feet too much;

● 'rambling' rather than being concise;

● giving away signs of being unprepared;

● exceeding allocated time for the presentation.

What to do

1 Decide what preparation is necessary

An update at the weekly meeting is unlikely to need the same degree of preparation as a talk at the annual conference.

Karen's habit of winging it came unstuck when she referred to Doreen, the CEO, as the secretary

By failing to prepare you are preparing to fail.

Benjamin Franklin

To help you decide how much to prepare:

● consider what you are trying to achieve as a result of the presentation or talk. If that outcome is worth achieving, then it follows that thorough preparation is worth doing;

● think of the consequences of something going wrong. The consequence of mistakes may be less important than in a talk to colleagues than in a presentation to a client;

● apply the 'that's good enough' rule once you know you have prepared appropriately;

● run your talk past a colleague or friend to test if you have prepared enough.

2 Get used to preparing at short notice

Where time is genuinely short, you can always do something to prepare:

- Use the planning structures in this book. They still work if you have less than the ideal amount of preparation time.

- Do not spend time memorising – instead speak from cue cards.

- Save time by looking for ready-made elements instead of creating completely new materials.

- Perhaps a friend or colleague has done something similar and asking their advice could reduce preparation time.

3 Practise 'off the cuff' speaking

Getting used to saying a few words 'off the cuff' may well help you to require less detailed preparation notes. For example, if you are in a meeting and are asked to say something with no notice, you can do so eloquently by using the ideas below:

- Use Secret 19 for guidance on speaking 'off the cuff'. You will learn how to keep a 'structure' in your head to marshal your thoughts and quickly organise what you want to say.

- See Secret 30, which helps you to overcome anxiousness.

- Use the body language tips. Secret 35 will help you to learn how to stand to feel confident and Secret 40 will show you how body language and voice will help you to be more credible.

- If you have time, jot down a few bullet points that you are going to cover. It is better than no planning at all.

Prepare properly and you will reap the rewards.

Your turn

For your next talk, speech or presentation, write down:

1   The three biggest benefits of getting it right.

2   The three worst consequences of getting it wrong.

3   The main things you need to do to prepare appropriately.

Resource for further learning

The Presenter's Edge: How to Unlock Your Inner Speaker (2016) by Gavin Meikle.

Concise and packed with practical tips. Especially ideal if you are short of time and want help fast.

2

What is the plan?

Secret 6: The four keys to success: outcome, rapport, attention and flexibility

These four keys to success are the pillars that support the other secrets in this book. Keeping them uppermost in your mind will help you stay on track throughout your preparation, practice and performance.

Why it matters

The four keys matter because:

- they are proven – every great speaker uses the four keys, even if they are unaware of it;
- if you fail to attend to any one of them, you will not succeed in convincing your audience;
- they offer a guide to dealing with many different audiences and situations;
- they enable you to have a plan but respond flexibly to what happens;
- once you grasp their importance, they will transform your ability to speak to audiences.

What to do

To deliver a great talk you need to do four things:

Jenny was keen to remember the *four keys to success in speaking,* but her reminder note seemed to distract the audience

1 Keep your outcome in mind

'Outcome thinking' as opposed to 'problem thinking' helps you to focus on your aim. Having a clear outcome in mind also lets you know when you have achieved what you set out to do. It also enables you to make better decisions whether preparing, practising or performing. This is because you are always checking potential actions against your desired outcome.

2 Build rapport

Building rapport is essential in order to persuade an audience to listen to your ideas. When you are speaking to groups you are influencing all the time. In fact the moment you walk on stage people are forming an impression of you, even before you speak. There is a true saying that goes; 'You cannot not influence.'

Before we can *lead* people towards our way of thinking, we need to *build and maintain rapport* with an audience. One of the secrets of building rapport is 'pacing' or matching the world of the audience, by starting your talk from where they are, rather than from your own viewpoint.

3　Pay attention

This is about noticing what is happening in the moment. It is about using your eyes and ears and is sometimes referred to as 'sensory awareness'. Keep your attention external, i.e. out on the audience, rather than in your head. By doing this, you gain valuable feedback about how your talk is being received. It enables you to see problems occurring and act before they develop. For example, by noticing audience reactions you can tell you if you are losing rapport or building it.

Keep your attention 'out there' to see problems early.

4　Be flexible

If your senses are telling you something is not working, then you need to do something differently. At the planning and practising stages, you need flexibility as you try things out. On stage, you may make fine adjustments as you go along or, sometimes, bigger changes in response to what is happening. For example, if you lose rapport with an audience, your first job is to get it back.

TIP

Keep your outcome in mind – but be flexible about how you get there.

Put the four keys into action to raise your speaking performance to the next level.

Your turn

Practise paying attention to rapport:

1 Next time you are in conversation, notice people's facial expressions.

2 Notice when rapport increases and decreases.

3 Do the same in a group. Identify people who are most in rapport and those who are not.

This will tune up your observation skills for the next time you are presenting to a group.

Resource for further learning

Influencing With Integrity: Management Skills for Communication and Negotiation (1995) by Genie Z. Laborde.

Learn in more depth about aspects covered in this Secret and how they apply also to communication skills such as sales and negotiation.

Secret 7: Look beyond your talk to get the outcome you want

As the saying goes, 'If you don't know where you're going, you might end up some place else.' This also applies to giving a talk, speech or presentation. You need to plan with the end in mind.

Why it matters

Reasons for clarifying your outcome:

- It gives you focus.
- You can imagine the end result – so you know what it is like when you get there.
- It influences your planning.
- It keeps you on track.
- It engages your unconscious mind to help you achieve it.

Look beyond the presentation to imagine what you want it to achieve

Your outcome governs everything else you do – so it needs to be clear.

What to do

Look beyond the talk

The talk is a means to an end. Look beyond your talk to see what you are really trying to achieve as a consequence of it. The example in the picture shows the aim is to be awarded a contract and a presentation to the client is required to make the case.

This example shows how an outcome often is not within your own control to achieve.

To understand this, it is helpful to understand goal-setting in sport.

There are three types of goals:

● **Outcome goals,** e.g. to win an Olympic Medal in the 400 metres.

● **Performance goals,** e.g. to be able to run a certain time for the distance.

● **Process goals,** e.g. a schedule of training activities.

The *outcome goal* is not within the control of the athlete because, if three people run faster, they do not win a medal.

However, by achieving an appropriate *performance goal,* the athlete will maximise the chances of the *outcome goal* being achieved. The *performance goal* is achieved by completing the *process goals.*

The same types of goals apply to talks, speeches and presentations.

As in the sports example, the outcomes of a talk are frequently not in your control. Irrespective of how good your pitch is, the client still may not award you the contract.

The summary below shows how the *possibility* of reaching the outcome can be increased by achieving *relevant objectives* for your talk. The objectives are, in turn, dependent on presenting *appropriate content.*

Here is an example:

Outcome goal (as a result of the presentation):

● The client will buy our products by placing an order – *not in your control,* but you can *increase the chances* by giving a convincing presentation.

Performance goals (objectives to be achieved by the end of the talk):

● By the end of our presentation, the client will understand our products and be convinced of their value to their business – *highly likely to be within your control* because the client will understand if you explain things well.

Process goals (content to be conveyed by the end of the talk):

● To explain products a, b and c and their value to the client's business – *totally within your control* because you can do that.

Therefore, while the *ideal* outcome may not be in your control, it is still a good place to start.

The next secret in the planning process will help you to:

- check outcomes to see *how realistic* they are;
- *make adjustments* so the final outcome for a talk is realistic;
- follow the steps required to plan your talk.

Your turn

Bring to mind an upcoming talk, speech or presentation.

1 Write your *outcome goal(s).*

2 Write your *performance goal(s).*

3 Write your *process goals(s).*

Resource for further learning

'TED's secret to great public speaking' by Chris Anderson, Head of TED (seven-minute video) on www.ted.com

Secret 8: Prepare your talk in six steps

It can be difficult to know where to start when planning a talk. However, by following these steps, you will be able to prepare in a systematic and time-efficient way. If you do nothing else, you will have the foundations of a good talk.

Why it matters

Following the six steps:

- means you start with the end in mind;
- keeps everything focused towards that desired outcome;

- means the content you need becomes more obvious;
- ensures your talk has a logical progression;
- makes selection of visuals straightforward;
- means you are less likely to miss things.

Follow the six steps to make it easier to plan your talk

Preparation can take longer than you think – so it pays to start early.

What to do

Just follow the six steps:

1   Think of the audience

'Designing a presentation without an audience in mind is like writing a love letter and addressing it:

"To Whom it May Concern".'

Ken Haemer, former Presentation Research Manager AT&T

With that in mind, ask yourself:

- Who will be in the audience?
- Why are they attending?
- What are their expectations?
- How many will be there?
- What is their level of knowledge about your topic?
- What might their attitude be towards your talk?

See Secret 9 for help identifying questions that might be on the minds of your audience.

2 Set outcomes and objectives

Just like planning a journey, first think about where you want to get to.

Set your desired outcome:

As emphasised in Secret 7, look beyond the talk.

For example, as a result of my talk:

- the team will work safely – they will demonstrate safe practices back at work;
- students will revise effectively for exams – they will use the techniques covered in the talk;
- the panel will make a decision to hire us – we will get a booking for a piece of work.

Set your objectives:

These are what you need to achieve in the talk in order to increase the chances of achieving your desired outcome.

There are three types of objectives:

- imparting knowledge;
- developing skills;
- changing attitudes or beliefs – usually intending to motivate people to action.

Useful phrasing for each of the three types of objectives could be:

By the end of my presentation the audience will:

- *understand or know . . .*

- *be able to do . . .*

- *commit to take action . . .*

Examples for each type of objective include:

- *Understanding:* the team will be able to explain the 10 safe working practices (i.e. they acquire knowledge, therefore they *understand*).

- *Being able to:* students will be able to use visual memory techniques (i.e. they are *able to do*).

- *Committing to action* (influencing attitudes and beliefs): the panel will be convinced that we can benefit their business and will decide to hire us.

3 Consider time and environment

What other factors will influence the plan for your talk?

Time:

- How long do you have?

- Does that include time for questions?

- Is there flexibility?

Environment:

- How big is the room?

- How are people seated?

- What equipment will be available?

Different set-ups will influence the *feel* of the occasion, such as making it formal or informal.

What can you do to get the set-up how you would ideally like it to be?

Stop!
Reality Check Before Continuing

Before going onto step 4, look at the triangle below, which shows the three s:
we have looked at so far. Make sure that your outcome and objectives can be
achieved with the given audience in that amount of time and in that environment.

If it looks unrealistic, then you need to make an adjustment. For example, if
there is too little time to achieve the outcome, you may need to make the
outcome more modest. Alternatively, you could request more time.

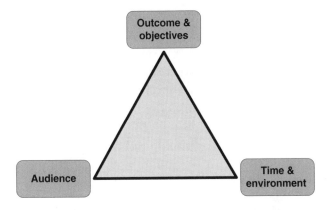

When you have completed the reality check on your triangle, proceed to step 4.

4 Structure content

Follow three steps:

● Brainstorm all potential content.

● Decide on content to keep or discard.

● Sequence the content in a logical 'story'.

See Secret 10 to learn how to structure your talk.

5 Design visuals

Now your content is sorted, you are in a position to decide on visuals. Ask
yourself, 'Do I actually need visuals?' because you may not.

...designing visuals.

...developing your talk as well as practising a fin-

...hile it is still being prepared will enable you to:

...works;

- come .... great phrases and ways of explaining ideas;
- get feedback;
- adjust and finalise the design;
- develop your script or guide notes.

Once your talk is ready, you can work on rehearsing your delivery. By practising repeatedly you can perfect your performance.

See Secret 33 for help with rehearsing.

Your turn

To become familiar with the steps:

- Have a go at a quick draft design of a talk using the first five steps.

Resource for further learning

The Presentation Book: How to Create it, Shape it and Deliver it! (2017) by Emma Ledden.

Chapter 4 'The six golden rules of Audience Focused Presenting' gives practical guidance on preparation.

Secret 9: Answer why, what, how, what if?

The four questions are based on the 4MAT System by Bernice McCarthy. The system is useful for structuring presentations in a way that the maximum number of people will understand. It works because members of your audience will be interested to a greater or lesser extent in the four different types of questions. By covering all four of them, you will appeal to most, if not all, of your audience.

Think through the four types of questions on the minds of any audience

Why it matters

Answering the four questions enables you to:

- plan content that will interest all, or most, people;
- structure content in an easy-to-follow sequence;
- reduce the risk of missing something vital from your talk;
- increase the chances of gaining buy-in;
- enhance the possibility of the audience taking actions you desire.

What to do

Put yourself in the minds of your audience and answer the questions below. Then, use those answers to help plan your talk as you follow the guidance in this Secret.

1 Why?

Imagine you are an audience member.

Ask yourself:

- 'Why should I listen?'
- 'Why is this topic important?'
- 'Why are you the right person to speak about it?'
- 'Why now?'

Think of more 'why' questions pertinent to your topic.

2 What?

Ask yourself:

- 'What's the key message?'
- 'What's the big idea?'
- 'What's the theory or model?
- 'What's the key information or evidence they need to hear?

Write down any more you can think of.

3 How?

Ask practical questions such as:

- 'How does it actually work?'
- 'Can you explain the practicalities?'
- 'How about some examples?'
- 'Can we see some evidence to support your theory?'
- 'Can you demonstrate it?'

4 What if?

There are two kinds of 'what if' questions:

(a) Negative 'what ifs'.

These are potential snags such as:

- Risks in what you are proposing;

- Flaws in your argument;

- Counter-examples that might dilute or refute your case;

- Exceptional circumstances when your guidance would not apply.

Such concerns might sound like this:

- 'What if there is not enough in the budget?'

- 'What if the scope of the project gets wider?'

- 'What if the client doesn't pay us on time?

- 'What if I don't have all that equipment?'

Think of your own questions specific to your situation.

TIP

Ask someone to play 'devil's advocate' and think of the most difficult questions that could come up.

(b) Positive 'what ifs'.

This is where people are already thinking about the future and imagining:

- where the information they have gleaned will be of use;

- the positive results of actions recommended;

- a vision of a successful future.

Such thoughts can translate into questions such as:

- 'Where will this be useful to me?"

- 'How can I apply this idea?

- 'What if I were to put this into practice?'

- 'When will we see the results?'

Decide which of the above questions apply to your topic and add more that relate to it.

Keep the answers and use them to help you decide what to include in your talk.

Think through the four questions before every talk and you will be well-prepared.

Your turn

Get used to using the four questions:

1 Think of a topic you have to speak about.
2 Think of all the questions that could be on the minds of the audience.
3 Write them down under the headings: Why? What? How? What if?
4 Use your answers as material for your talk.

Resource for further learning

The 4MAT System: Teaching to Learning Styles with Right/Left Mode Techniques (1981) by Bernice McCarthy.

Useful if you want to explore the system in depth and is helpful for applications to teaching and learning.

Secret 10: Structure your talk so it makes logical sense

You may have been to talks that seemed disorganised. There really is no need for this because, by using the logical structure below, you can make it flow like a story every time.

Why it matters

If your flow is not logical:

● people may find it disjointed;
● people may have difficulty following it;

- your key message may get lost;

- it is unlikely that you will captivate and inspire your audience;

- they may lose confidence in you.

The team loved Brian, but they wished he was more logical

What to do

Use the following structure, based on the 4MAT System by Bernice McCarthy. It follows the questions we looked at in Secret 9: *Why? What? How? What If?* You can use your answers to those questions to feed into your plan as you work through the following guidance.

1   Short *What*?

This is a one-liner that tells the audience what the talk is about, for example:

- 'I will explain how our latest Health and Safety Policy will impact the way we work.'

- 'I am going to give you a project update and highlight the key issues still to be resolved.'

- 'I'm here to share our targets for the coming year and show how you can help to achieve them.'

2   Why?

This is all about:

- building rapport;
- creating curiosity;
- increasing motivation to listen.

Start from where they are, then lead towards the outcome.

- Tell them why it is important – give reasons to listen.
- Ask rhetorical questions to build curiosity.
- Explain the problem.
- Spell out consequences of not addressing the issue.
- Highlight benefits of resolving the problem.

Use a linking phrase to transition into the next section, such as:

- 'Therefore, today I will share with you what we are doing about this . . . '

3   What?

Your key message. This is the main part of your content. It can include:

- the big idea;
- the theory;
- the main concept.

4   How?

Supporting pillars. Explain how your main idea works in practice and provide supporting evidence, such as practical examples, case studies or a demonstration.

You can see the structure on the next page.

It is like creating a storyboard.

The structure enables you to:

- break down your content into chunks of information;

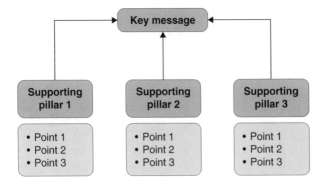

● arrange those chunks into an easy-to-follow sequence.

Three has impact:

● 'Here are three ways to be more productive.'

● 'The three reasons we need to take action are . . . '

● 'The three most common mistakes companies make are . . . '

It is easier to see how the structure works when we add some content, as in the example overleaf on the topic of health.

5   What if?

There are two sides to the 'what if' question: the negative and the positive.

(a) The negative 'what ifs'

Think in advance of possible audience concerns and address them at this point.

● 'What if this happens . . . ?'

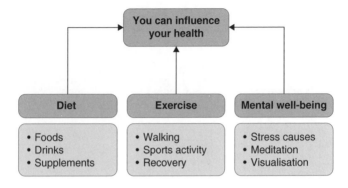

- 'What if it doesn't work . . . ?'

- 'What about exceptional circumstances . . . ?'

(b) Questions from the audience – this is an ideal place for a question-time session

Now invite questions and ideas from the audience if you wish to.

(c) Positive 'what ifs'

Finish your talk with a positive ending:

- *Summarise key message*

  Repeat your key message to leave it fresh in their memories.

- *Make your call to action*

  If you want them to do something, then this is the time to ask.

- *Outline the future new reality*

Explain what will happen as a result of taking the requested action.

Paint a picture of what will be different.

There is more help with the three stages above in Secret 60 End on a high, not a whimper.

Your turn

1   Think of a talk you have coming up.

2   Use this structure to draft your talk with a logical flow.

3   Write main ideas on sticky notes so you can move them about until it works.

Resource for further learning

Resonate: Present Visual Stories that Transform Audiences (2010) by Nancy Duarte.

Chapters 6 and 7 give you plenty of guidance on structuring talks.

Secret 11: Vary the rhythm

Just like a piece of music that sounds great at the start, if a talk goes on much the same without a change, we soon lose interest. But, if you make sure your talks have plenty of variation in *content, method of delivery* and *pace,* then your audience will stay engaged throughout.

Why it matters

● Sameness gets tedious and tiring for the audience.

● When people become bored, they 'zone out' and stop paying attention.

● With variation, you can evoke positive feelings such as curiosity and excitement.

● A varied rhythm makes key messages more memorable.

● By changing the rhythm, you can increase impact.

● Impact increases the chances of the audience taking the action you desire.

What to do

Use ideas from the 'Start, Middle, End' chart, overleaf, to vary the rhythm.

Varying the rhythm makes your talk more enjoyable for the audience

Start	Middle			End
Start where they are	Contrasts	Stories	Metaphors	Summary
Create curiosity		Logic Emotion		Call-to-action
Grab attention	Seeing	Hearing	Feeling	Describe the new reality
Pacing and leading	Memorable words and pictures			
	Humour Wow moments Energy spikes			
	Challenge thinking Show need to change			
	Consequences of not changing			
	Make it easy to step on board with the change			

Three important things to do:

1 Vary the content

● *Keep your subject moving* – do not dwell longer than necessary on one point.

- *Give key ideas* – rather than great detail, unless there is reason to add detail.

- *Make strong links* – between one piece of content and the next.

2 Vary the method

Make it multi-sensory

People will have different preferences for how they learn. When you make your talk multi-sensory by varying the methods used, you will appeal to the preferences of more people more of the time.

You might include:

- *seeing* photographs, graphs, flowcharts, diagrams, videos;

- *hearing* stories, case studies, jokes, examples, facts, music;

- *saying:* asking people to discuss an aspect of the talk with the person sitting next to them;

- *Doing:* asking them to solve a puzzle, write something or collaborate on an activity with another person or group.

TIP

Beware of using only methods that match your own preferences – keep it varied.

---

3 Vary the pace

As you vary content and methods, you will find the pace naturally changes. However, you can also do much to enhance this through changing your own pace and energy.

- *Slow down* to add drama.

- *Speed up* to add excitement.

- *Pause* to let points sink in.

- *Make it lively* to keep it light and entertaining.
- *Make it serious* to emphasise important points.

Your turn

Enhance the rhythm of an upcoming talk:

1 Look through your draft of an upcoming talk as if it were a piece of music.

2 Identify where you already have interesting variation of content, method and pace.

3 Make a note of any parts where you do not.

4 Use the guidance in this Secret to help you think of ideas to enhance those parts.

5 Select only the best of those ideas and incorporate them into your plan.

Resource for further learning

'The transformative power of classical music' by Benjamin Zander at TED2008 (20-minute video), www.ted.com

Great example of a talk with excellent variation that keeps people engaged.

Secret 12: Start from where the audience are

When a speaker is too enthusiastic about their idea, it can 'turn off' an audience. Before introducing your ideas, you need to acknowledge how your audience may be thinking or feeling. This will show that you understand them and, as a result, they are more likely to be open to your ideas.

Why it matters

Sometimes talks start with enthusiastic phrases such as:

- 'I am very excited to tell you about x . . . .'

- 'I have a great idea that is going to change how we do things . . . '

- 'I am delighted to tell you about a new way to do x . . . '

When what you are saying is at odds with the feelings of the audience, it can widen the gap between you and them. The speaker might be excited, but the audience have yet to see a reason why they should be equally ecstatic.

Derek wondered why the staff were not as excited as he was, but he ploughed on anyway

What to do

1   Start from where they are

Instead of launching off into your topic, *put yourself in their shoes.* Use opening phrases that match the audience's current experience, concerns and needs.

TIP

Match the audience in order to build rapport.

Once you *match* the audience, you will be better placed to *lead* them into your topic. This approach to being more influential is often called 'pacing *and leading*.'

● **Pacing**

When what we say matches how the audience think or feel, we are *pacing their model of the world,* i.e. acknowledging their current reality. Pacing can occur not only through our words, but through our voice or body language. For example, we might use a serious voice to match a concerned audience.

Joseph O'Connor and John Seymour, authors of *Introducing NLP,* liken this to building a bridge: 'You cannot lead someone over a bridge without building it first.'

● **Leading**

Leading takes the audience in the direction you want them to go. They are more likely to listen to what you have to say if, first, you have built rapport through adequate pacing.

2   Prepare to pace and lead your audience

    (a) Think about who will be there

        ● In what capacity are they attending?

        ● Is attendance voluntary or compulsory?

        ● Is it an audience of experts?

        ● Is your topic new to them?

    (b) Ask yourself: *'What may they be thinking or feeling about my talk?'*

        ● 'I hope this is going to be worth the time out of my diary.'

        ● 'We've had a lot of challenges on this project.'

        ● 'I hope we get some useful guidance.'

    (c) Write opening phrases that match their thoughts and feelings

Use *'yes-sets'*

'Yes-sets' are statements that are true for the audience and to which they will mentally say 'yes'. They will help you to start your talk from the *audience's viewpoint* rather than your own.

- 'I know you are all busy people so I appreciate you taking time to be here.'

- 'As you may have noticed, there have been some problems with the new system.'

- 'Some of you have experienced real difficulties as a result of this.'

    N.B. Avoid saying things that apply only to some audience members because you will alienate others. Instead, mainly use phrases that include *everyone,* such as: *'For some of you, this is all too familiar, while for others it may be completely new.'* This is a good pacing statement because it includes the entire audience.

(d) Use a linking phrase to *lead* into your talk

Link the *pacing* statements into the *leading* statements. This shows the audience how what you have just said relates to what you are about to say. It also makes the transition smooth between the 'yes-sets' and your next statements.

Linking phrases:

- 'Therefore, I will share with you what we are doing about this.'

- 'In order to address these issues, I'd like to outline . . . '

- 'It's because of these problems that we now need to do x, y, z. . . '

3 Make sure you do enough pacing

The big mistake: trying to lead your audience too quickly

Tom Bird and Jeremy Cassell, authors of *The Leaders' Guide to Presenting*

Bird and Cassell give the example of presenting to a group of 'disgruntled employees on yet another change programme'. In this instance, they suggest that you may need to *extend the time* you take on pacing. If you move on too quickly, it is possible that the audience may feel that you have only 'paid lip service to their concerns'.

> **TIP**
>
> Look at audience reactions. If they are with you, then you will see nods and facial expressions that let you know you are building rapport.

Your turn

1   Think of a presentation coming up or a topic you might speak on.

2   Follow steps 1 to 3 above, to write opening phrases to match your audience.

3   Practise introducing your talk by using these phrases.

Resource for further learning

The Leader's Guide to Presenting: How to Use Soft Skills to Get Hard Results (2017) by Tom Bird and Jeremy Cassell.

Focuses on presenting to motivate staff and build relationships. Chapter 6 gives detail on pacing and leading.

Secret 13: Show the audience *what is* and *what could be*

For people to take action they need to understand where it will take them. When you *show them the difference* between *what is* and *what could be,* the *contrast* between the two can increase motivation to listen to what you have to say. It works because you awaken people to just what could be possible in the future compared to where they are now.

Why it matters

Some people are motivated by the thought of getting *away from* something they do not like such as getting *away* from problems, *avoiding* hassle. Such a person springs into action when the consequences of *not* acting are *bad,* such as when a pressing deadline is missed.

Others are more motivated by the thought of moving *towards* something, such as a goal. This person takes action because of the thought of how *good* the result of *taking action* will be.

Research by Rodger Bailey found that, in a work context, around 40 per cent of people have a 'toward' pattern and 40 per cent have an 'away from' pattern.

When you start a talk by *highlighting the gap* between how *bad* the current situation *is* compared with how *good* the future *could be,* you motivate *both* kinds of people. Not only that, but the remaining 20 per cent, who typically have an *equally* 'towards' and 'away from' pattern, are motivated too.

By contrasting 'what is' with 'what could be', Dave certainly got the team fired up

What to do

1   Start with *what is*

Talk about the *current state*; how things are now. This may be a problem the audience recognise. They will realise that you understand their world and you will build rapport with them. See Secret 12 for more help on starting talks.

2 Show them what *could be*

Explain the benefits of getting *away from* the *current state* and *moving towards* the *desired state* of *'what could be'.*

In her book *Resonate,* Nancy Duarte likens this to getting people to join you on an adventure:

To create the call to adventure, put forth a memorable big idea that conveys what could be. This is the moment when the audience see the stark contrast between what is and what could be for the first time.

TIP

Highlight the contrast between 'what is' and 'what could be' *early* in your talk.

When you highlight big contrasts, it heightens the motivation.

In my talk at TEDxHull, only a very small percentage of the audience said 'yes' to the question: '*How many people here would say they can draw?'* This established *'what is'.* I then showed them some of my cartoon pictures and asked if they would like to be able to draw like that. The big *contrast* between *'what is'* and *'what could be'* was established.

Here are other examples of contrasts:

- Current performance compared with potential performance.
- The hassle of how we do it now versus how much easier it could be.
- Existing problems compared with future solutions.
- Current pain contrasted with future gains.
- Poor skills now versus excellent future skills.
- *'What if we don't?'* versus '*What if we do?'*

3   Structure your talk to bridge the gap

Your talk then becomes a journey in which you guide people from *what is* to *what could be.* Use the Secrets in this book to help you with planning that journey.

Influencing language:

In her book *Words That Change Minds,* Shelle Rose Charvet suggests language to influence people with a '*toward*' pattern includes: *attain, obtain, have, get, include, achieve.*

For those with an '*away from*' pattern, she recommends: *avoid, prevent, eliminate, solve, get rid of.*

Use both kinds of words to ensure that you appeal to everyone.

The desired state may not be achieved by the end of the talk. It may be that the call-to-action is the first step on their journey.

Your turn

For your next talk or presentation:

1   Use the guidance above to write an introduction that highlights the gap between '*what is*' and '*what could be.*'

2   Have a practice run-through by just talking it through to yourself.

3   Make any refinements needed.

Resource for further learning

Resonate: Present Visual Stories that Transform Audiences (2010) by Nancy Duarte.

Chapter 2 'Lessons from Myths and Movies' provides great ideas for contrasting 'what is' with 'what could be' and more.

Secret 14: How to motivate people to act

For people to take action, they must *feel* they want, or need, to do it. If there is a big gap between how they currently feel and how you want them to feel, then you need to help them to bridge it. Start from *where they are* and *lead them gradually to where you want them to go.*

Why it matters

People rarely change their feelings about something quickly. Therefore, usually, you need to take the audience *gradually* from how they feel currently to how you want them to feel.

By identifying how the audience might feel at the start you can:

- identify the gap between how they feel now and how you want them to feel by the end;
- do a reality check to see if that is achievable in your talk; if it is not realistic, decide what to do;
- begin your talk from where they are;
- plan content that evokes the feelings that will help to win them over;
- motivate them to take your desired actions.

Even though they had yet to hear about it, Mary's team took an instant dislike to the new system

What to do

Plan content that moves people from how they feel at the start to how you want them to feel by the end.

Help people move from how they currently feel to how you want them to feel

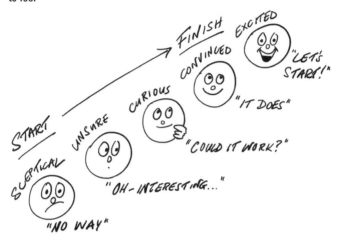

Make a note of your answers to the following questions, then use those answers to help plan your talk.

1   What do you want them to *do* as a result of your talk?

You might, for example, want them to apply some knowledge, put a skill into practice, support a cause, follow a procedure, take further interest in your topic, support you in urgent action or use a new system.

2   How would they need to *feel* to be motivated to take that action?

It could be one or more feelings, such as shocked, worried, concerned, curious, intrigued, excited, inspired, confident or motivated.

3   What would they need to *believe* that would evoke those feelings?

● 'If we don't do something quickly, we're in trouble.'

● 'This is serious.'

- 'This idea has a lot of merit.'

- 'We can make a difference here.'

- 'We've done it before so we can do it again.'

- 'A small action will make a big difference.'

4   Assess the gap – how big is it?

What is the gap between how the audience currently feel and how you want them to feel?

That gap could be:

- big – most of them will be against this idea – an uphill task;

- moderate – they could be persuaded if the case is strong;

- small – it will be like pushing at an open door – they will all go for it.

TIP

If the gap is too large to be bridged, ask yourself what you could realistically achieve.

---

5   What do they need to *see* and *hear* to bridge the gap?

What could start getting people to think differently?

- If they are sceptical, what would make them *doubt* their own view? Perhaps a surprising fact or a shocking statistic.

- What would make them really *curious*? For example an intriguing proposition.

- What would *convince* them? It could be stories that evoke emotions.

- Once they are convinced, what can you say to make them really *motivated?* Perhaps you could highlight the difference their support will make.

Now use those answers to help you write down your ideas for content that will bridge the gap.

6 In what *sequence* is that content best presented?

Arrange the content in a logical order to take people from their *current feelings* to *desired feelings.* See Secret 10 for more help on structuring your talk.

Your turn

Think of an upcoming talk and write down answers to the following:

1 What do you want the audience to do as a result of your talk?

2 How would they need to feel to make it likely they would do that?

3 What do they need to believe?

4 What do they currently feel and believe?

5 What content would move them towards feeling how you want them to?

6 What is the best sequence for that content?

Resource for further learning

The Leader's Guide to Presenting: How to Use Soft Skills to Get Hard Results (2017) by Tom Bird and Jeremy Cassell.

Chapter 7 'Why structure is so important and the key principles' provides guidance specifically on a 'structure to engage and motivate the audience.'

Secret 15: Use Aristotle's three pillars of persuasion

In the fourth century BC, Aristotle wrote in his book *Rhetoric* that a persuasive speech is supported by three pillars: ethos – being credible and of good character; logos – being logical and factual; and pathos – having emotional appeal. Each pillar is important because people are rarely persuaded by just one of them. Incorporate all three and you will greatly enhance the chances of the audience being convinced by what you say.

Why it matters

It pays to use all three for the following reasons:

- **Ethos** conveys your expertise and that you are trustworthy and knowledgeable. This makes it likely that the audience will respect you, see you as credible and have confidence in you.

- **Logos** is about appealing to the head by using reasoned argument and solid evidence to back up your message and any claims you may make.

- **Pathos** helps you to appeal to the heart. For example, using relevant stories gives rise to feelings by triggering emotions that cause the audience to support your message.

- If you miss one out, you are reducing the persuasive power of your talk.

- Using all three will support your case in a balanced way, like three legs on a stool.

- You heighten impact by including all three.

- You will appeal to the different kinds of people in an audience.

Roger's logic seemed faultless, but somehow the team were still not persuaded

What to do

Apply all three of Aristotle's pillars of persuasion.

Ethos: establish your credibility, authority and character

1 Communicate your authority to speak

If being introduced or asked for a biography; write a few lines in the third person. You might include relevant experience, your title and qualifications.

TIP

Be introduced, if possible, rather than introduce yourself because it increases your credibility.

---

2 Use credible sources

Refer to credible research using objective information from reputable people and organisations. Explain your case in an impartial way to show you are unbiased.

3 Show you have something in common

Use language appropriate to the audience's field of expertise. Share experiences you have in common. People like others who are similar to themselves.

Research such as that by Robert Cialdini shows people are more easily persuaded when they like you.

Logos: use logic and reason

Avoid rambling and vagueness, instead be logical and clear.

1 Give facts

Use evidence in the form of indisputable facts and statistics. Graphs, charts and diagrams are ideal for conveying such information.

2 Use logical argument

Ensure that your case makes complete logical sense. Give the rationale behind any recommendations you make.

3 Structure the whole talk in logical steps

Use easy-to-follow steps in the flow of your talk. Signpost where you are going to help people follow the journey.

Pathos: appeal to emotions

Use the following methods to trigger emotions that help to convince people of your message.

1 Use stories, analogies and metaphors

Stories fire the imagination and can elicit every kind of emotion. Analogies and metaphors make ideas easy to understand, e.g. 'this a rollercoaster ride'.

2 Use vivid language

Bring ideas to life by using vivid language. Paint pictures with your words and you will help the audience to engage emotionally. Help them to *see* the pictures, *hear* the sounds and get a *feel* for what you are talking about.

3 Show powerful pictures

A picture can spark an emotional reaction. Think of how people respond to photographs of children or animals.

Use all three of Aristotle's secrets to persuade your audience.

Your turn

1 Write a few lines about yourself that establishes your credentials. Give it to whoever will introduce you, use it to introduce yourself or to write a brief biography.

2 Find an example of facts or data from one of your presentations. Now come up with a real story or anecdote to back it up.

3 Before your next talk, check to see that you have included Aristotle's three pillars.

Resource for further learning

The Art of Rhetoric by Aristotle (1992), Penguin Classics, translated by Hugh Lawson-Tancred.

Useful if you want an in-depth understanding of this topic.

Secret 16: Remember, the title is more than just a title

The title may be the last thing on your mind when you are busy preparing a talk. However, coming up with a powerful title can have great benefits.

Why it matters

A powerful title will help you to:

● get people curious;

● motivate people to listen;

● create impact before you start;

● 'frame' your talk so people understand its context;

● spell out the benefits of listening.

Although it was somewhat accurate, Jeff was starting to regret asking Pam to come up with a new title for his weekly update

What to do

Compare the following presentation titles:

- 'Health and Safety Update'
- 'How the New Safety Laws Will Change the Way You Work'

It is easy to see how they prompt different reactions. The second one lets you know something of the benefits of attending the presentation.

Structure and elements of titles

1 Title and subtitle

A title and subtitle is a great format because it allows you to do so much.

The following examples are from talks at the London Business Forum:

- 'Yes: Secrets from the science of persuasion' – Steve Martin

- 'Gravitas: How to speak so others listen' – Caroline Goyder

- 'Make your brain work: Top tips to boost performance' – Amy Brann

They show how you can create a catchy main title, and then the subtitle does the 'legwork' of stating the benefits of attending.

Get the benefits of your talk into your title whenever you can.

2 Use 'How' titles

The following TED talk titles show how effective the 'how' and 'how to' title can be for talks:

- 'How your brain decides what is beautiful'– Anjan Chatterjee (TEDMED 2016)

- 'How to design a library that makes kids want to read' – Michael Bierut (TEDNYC 2017)

- 'How to truly listen' – Evelyn Glennie (TED2003)

3 Use 'Question' titles

Making the title a question can be powerful, as shown in these TED talk examples.

- 'What if we ended the injustice of bail?' – Robin Steinberg (TED2018)

- 'What's it like to be a robot?' – Leila Takayama (TEDxPaloAlto 2017)

- 'What happens in your brain when you pay attention?' – Mehdi Ordikhani-Seyedlar (TED2017)

4 Use 'Why?' titles

'Why' sparks our curiosity, as the examples below show:

- 'Why jobs of the future won't feel like work' – David Lee (TED@ UPS 2017)

- 'Why glass towers are bad for city life – and what we need instead' – Justin Davidson (TEDNYC 2017)

- 'Why should anyone work here? How to attract top talent' – Gareth Jones (London Business Forum 2016)

How to write a great title

1   Write a lot of titles

This will increase the chances of coming up with a great one.

TIP

Do not edit or discount titles, just keep writing until you have a long list.

---

2   Check and adjust your titles

Most of the time you need to experiment with wording to get a good title.

- Keep the strong words.

- Get rid of or replace weaker or unnecessary words.

- Juggle words and phrases to find what works best.

- Create a shortlist of good titles.

3   Test your shortlist of titles on people

You get valuable feedback by noticing someone's instinctive reaction. You can then modify titles as a result.

What to be careful about

Shorter titles are not always better.

Instinctively, one might think that a short snappy title is best. However, I found many talk titles with up to around 13 words and they sound great. This is because longer titles can explain what the talk will do for you.

Your turn

Write a great title for your next talk:

1 Think of a presentation you have coming up.

2 Write at least 10 possible titles, regardless of whether they sound any good.

3 Play around with wording and come up with a shortlist.

4 Test them on someone.

5 Make your final choice.

Resource for further learning

Go to the TED website to see the online library of talks. Browse through the titles to get ideas for your own titles: www.ted.com

Secret 17: Get creative by using the power of your unconscious mind

To come up with the best ideas for our talk, or solve a complex problem in planning it, we would be wise to harness the power of our unconscious mind. This is because of the vast processing power of the unconscious mind compared with conscious thinking.

Scott Barry Kaufman has researched creativity at the University of Pennsylvania. He recommends a four-step creative process that will set your unconscious mind to work on your talk when you are not even thinking about it.

Why it matters

The conscious mind is restricted in creative ability compared with the unconscious:

● **Conscious 'hare brain' thinking has its limitations:**

In *Hare Brain Tortoise Mind,* Guy Claxton writes: 'Deliberate thinking, d-mode, works well when the problem it is facing is easily conceptualised.'

So it works fine for problems needing logical thought, but it has limitations for resolving complex issues. This is because of the small amount of information we can keep in our conscious minds at one moment. George Miller's research found we can hold around *only seven* items of information in our working memory at once.

Conversely:

● **Creative insights occur with a more relaxed 'tortoise mind':**

Claxton describes this way of thinking as: 'Less purposeful and clear-cut, more playful, leisurely and dreamy.'

Our mind might be wandering when we sit looking at the sea. This slower mental register can process huge amounts of information. Colin Martindale's research at the University of Maine demonstrates that creativity is linked to this lower-focused mental activity.

Jim hadn't even been thinking about his speech when the most brilliant idea popped into his head

What to do

Kaufman identified four stages to tap into the power of your unconscious mind: preparation, incubation, illumination and verification.

The four steps are below, with guidance on how to apply them when planning a talk.

1   Preparation – work on your talk *consciously* to prime your unconscious mind

The unconscious mind needs to know what it needs to work on. Prime your unconscious mind by writing down:

- desired outcomes;

- initial ideas;

- aspects on which you would like creative ideas.

2   Incubation – go about your normal business – let your mind wander

To enable your unconscious mind to work on your talk:

- forget about your talk for a while;

- take walks or do other activities;

- just mull it over now and then when in a contemplative state.

You need to allow time gaps for your unconscious to get to work.

One key reason that incubation works is because of our reticular activating system (RAS). This bundle of nerves filters out information we do not need and alerts us to information that is helpful.

3   Illumination – when you get those lightbulb moments write them down

This is where you are apt to get insights. You never know when they will occur, but make a note of them when they do.

Write down insights when they occur

4 Verification – *consciously* work on your talk and test those lightbulb ideas

Resume working on your talk.

- Look back at your lightbulb moments.

- Test them with a *critical mind* to see how useful they are.

- Incorporate the useful ideas into your plan.

- Review and identify what needs sorting next.

Repeat the four steps as necessary as you develop your talk.

Make it a habit of allowing your unconscious mind to help you. It will maximise your chances of creating outstanding talks.

Your turn

1 Write down where and when is best for you to work on a talk in depth.

2 When you plan your next talk, decide when you will have time gaps where you forget about it for a while.

3 Then, as ideas naturally occur to you, just write them down.

Resource for further learning

Hare Brain Tortoise Mind: Why Intelligence Increases When You Think Less (1999) by Guy Claxton.

For an in-depth look at research on modes of thinking, especially intuition.

Secret 18: Turn off your computer to plan your talk

It may be tempting to use slide software such as PowerPoint to plan a talk. However, when people do this they are not truly designing, but following the programme they are using. Typically, this means working in a *linear* way, typing points into slide after slide. It is easy to stray into this when you are meant to be planning the talk. This way of working can hamper the focused thinking and creative approach required for good design. As mentioned in Secret 8, it is best to create slides *after* you have planned your talk.

Why it matters

Garr Reynolds, author of *Presentation Zen,* advises that, when designing a presentation, you need to 'create a stillness of mind for yourself'. He emphasises that this is 'something that's hard to do while puttering around on the computer'.

It is important to use a planning method that:

- enables you to see the whole picture at once;
- helps you to see links and relationships;
- enables you to focus deeply;
- helps you to think clearly and creatively;
- encourages flexibility and allows you to amend ideas easily;
- results in you creating a kind of storyboard for your talk.

What to do

Use good old-fashioned pencil, pens and paper along with sticky notes that you can move around. You may also like to have a whiteboard or flipchart to display your ideas as you work on them.

Turn off your computer and turn on your brain.

Split your planning into three steps:

Step 1 Write your content ideas on sticky notes

Keep the desired outcome of your talk visible as you brainstorm possible content. This is where you use 'divergent thinking', i.e. thinking widely and considering anything that comes to mind.

> Write lots of ideas and you increase the chances of coming up with a brilliant one

- Write one idea per sticky note.

- Keep your mind open and do not edit at this stage.

- Set a time limit – it can help you keep up momentum.

Step 2 Structure into key messages and supporting pillars to make a storyboard

In this stage, your thinking can be more convergent as you narrow down and organise your ideas.

- Group related ideas together.

- Get rid of ideas that do not fit.

Using sticky notes makes it easy to move ideas around

- Create a structure of key messages and supporting ideas to make your storyboard.

See Secret 10 for help on getting the structure and sequence right.

Step 3 Think of ideas for slides and place them in a sequence

---

TIP

Ask yourself: 'Would my talk be better delivered without any slides?'

If you use slides, remember that you do not need one for everything you say, as mentioned in Secret 20. Add slides only where they help you make your point.

Keeping everything visible makes it easier to organise and check your sequence

- Look at your key messages and supporting ideas.

- Think what visuals people would need to see to help you convey your points such as data, pictures, statistics, charts.

- Draw your ideas for visuals on sticky notes.

- A simple rough sketch will suffice.

- Write a key word if it helps.

- Keep to one idea per sticky note.

Now turn your computer on and create your slides and any support material such as handouts.

Your turn

Think of a talk that is coming up or a typical topic you might talk about:

1   Use the three steps above to plan it.

2   Check your plan with a colleague to get feedback.

3   Make adjustments to your plan.

Resource for further learning

Presentation Zen: Simple Ideas on Presentation Design and Delivery (2011) by Garr Reynolds.

Chapter 3 'Planning Analog' gives tips on planning without the computer.

Secret 19: How to structure a talk 'off-the-cuff'

Have you ever been asked to speak with little or no notice? Perhaps you were unexpectedly asked to update a team on a project. Or maybe you were called upon to give an urgent briefing.

In such situations, you need to marshal your thoughts quickly. Under pressure, it is easy to get information out of sequence and even completely miss out something vital.

The secret is having a structure in your head that will convey any information in an easy-to-follow sequence.

Why it matters

- If you speak in a muddled way, it reflects badly on yourself.
- Being able to organise your thoughts quickly gives you confidence.
- Once you have a method, you can use it time and again.

What to do

Improvise *but with a structure* on which to hang all your ideas.

> *Just remind yourself of the four questions: Why? What? How? What if?*

These are the same questions we looked at in the 4MAT System in Secrets 9 and 10.

Nigel's ability to speak 'off the cuff' always impressed colleagues; little did they know, he had a 'magic' structure in his head!

Being able to speak 'off-the-cuff' is easier with a structure already in your head.

Let's work through an example.

Imagine you are in a team meeting. Without any warning, someone asks you to give an update on the progress of a project. Everyone looks towards you.

Instead of panicking and saying the first thing that comes into your head, just bring to mind those four questions: Why? What? How? and What if?

All you need to do is *hang your content on those questions.* Your explanation will be organised, logical and easy to understand.

Follow this sequence.

The points suggested below are examples. In practice, you may leave out some and add others.

1. **Give them a 'one-liner' that sums up what you are speaking about**

   This is sometimes called a 'short what' because, in a sentence, it tells the audience *what* you are about to explain.

2. **Why?**

   - Why is the project happening?
   - Explain what problems the project is addressing.
   - Why does it matter to these people?

3. **What?**

   - What is the big idea of the project?
   - What is the key message they need to remember?
   - If you need to break it down, go for three main ideas, if possible.
   - Mention other relevant information in support.

4. **How?**

   - How does the project work in practice?
   - Give examples to bring it to life.
   - Where are you now with the project?
   - Add other relevant information about the practicalities.

5. **What if?**

   (a) **Problems and risks**

   - What problems have come up?
   - What steps have been taken to solve those problems?
   - What issues can you foresee?
   - How will you prevent those or get around them?

   (b) **Any questions or comments?**

   - Invite questions.

   (c) **Repeat your key message**

   - Remind them of the message to take away.

- Write it on a flipchart or whiteboard.

(d) Call-to-action

- Remind everyone of any actions you want them to take.

(e) Paint a picture of the future new reality

End on a positive note:

- What is happening next?

- Refer to the short and longer term.

- What positive differences will it all make?

- Thank them for listening.

TIP

Use the words why, what, how at the start of those sections to signal where you are.

Once you get used to the pattern, it becomes second nature.

Your turn

Have a go at explaining a topic or a project 'off the cuff' to practise.

You might like to:

- record your voice and play it back;

- ask a colleague to listen and give feedback.

1 Write down the four questions as prompts: Why? What? How? What if?

2 Now just go for it; start talking by using each question as a prompt, as in the example above.

3 Discuss how it went or review your recording.

Resource for further learning

Presenting Magically – Transforming Your Stage Presence With NLP (2016) by Tad James and David Shephard.

Covers numerous aspects of presenting; see Chapter 14 for more guidance on the 4MAT System.

3

A visual paints
a 1000 words

Secret 20: Your slides are not your presentation

People often speak as if the slides are the presentation itself:

- 'Would you like to borrow my presentation?'
- 'My presentation is on a memory stick.'
- 'Unfortunately, I will miss your presentation so can you email it to me?'

This way of thinking leads to a slide-led presentation and diminishes the role of the presenter to that of simply narrating the slides.

Instead – think of yourself as the presentation with your slides in support.

Why it matters

Your presentation is way more than just a set of slides because your personal impact as a speaker is what will influence people most.

Regarding the slide set as the presentation often results in:

- the speaker feeling they need a slide for everything they have to say;
- too many slides, which often is draining for the audience;
- people visibly slumping when they realise that there are numerous slides to get through;

- boring the audience: many are bored with slides, even though not all slides are boring;
- emphasis on slides which can dilute the speaker's personal impact;
- reliance on slides which ignores many other ways of engaging people.

There is no need for a slide for everything you want to say because you are there to say it.

If your presentation was a just a set of slides, there would be no need for you to speak

What to do

1   Remember that *you* are the presentation not the slides

Instead of giving your slides 'top billing', use your energy, voice, gestures and body language to convey your message. Then refer to your slides to support what you are saying.

One of the most popular TED talks has no slides. In his talk 'Do Schools Kill Creativity?', Sir Ken Robinson gets his message across through his personal presence and impact.

Having fewer slides has more impact because those you do show stand out more.

2 Create your talk first

If you start creating slides while planning your talk, you will, almost certainly, end up with more than you need. This is because of the temptation to have everything on a slide.

TIP

Get your storyline right before even thinking about slides.

When you complete the storyline first, you are in a better position to step back and consider the slides you need. See Secrets 8, 9 and 10 for help with creating your talk.

3 Now create *only* the slides you need to support you

Think carefully about where a slide will make a difference. Be selective so that the slides you do create add the most value. See Secret 22 for help with slide design.

Create only slides that make a difference.

What if I like to have everything on slides so I don't forget it?

Slides are for the audience's benefit, but there might be a place where you do include a slide to avoid forgetting something vital. However, this should be the exception. As a rule, it's best to use other ways of remembering e.g. cue cards or notes.

Your turn

For your next presentation, plan like this in order to end up with fewer slides.

Plan your talk on paper, with sticky notes or on a whiteboard using the guidance in Secret 18.

Resource for further learning

The Presentation Book: How to create it, shape it and deliver it (2013) by Emma Ledden.

Chapter 6 'The Audience Focused Presenting way' gives guidance on 'presenter-led' rather than 'slide-led' presenting.

Secret 21: Use strong visuals to make it memorable

You want your talk to be remembered and research proves that showing visuals increases memorability.

For example, in *The Mindmap Book* Tony and Barry Buzan refer to the work of Raymond Nickerson who showed subjects 10,000 *vivid* pictures. On seeing such *striking* pictures, subjects, when tested, were able to say with *99.9 per cent accuracy* if they had seen a given picture before. Therefore, use vivid and striking pictures to maximise memorability.

Why it matters

By using vivid visuals in a talk:

● you can get a point across instantly;

● messages are easily absorbed and remembered;

● impact is increased;

● talks are easier to follow;

● you accelerate the rate at which you can convey ideas and information;

● you can make your talk more entertaining and enjoyable.

The capacity of recognition memory for pictures is almost limitless . . .

Lionel Standing

'Learning 10,000 Pictures', *The Quarterly Journal of Experimental Psychology,* **Vol. 25, Issue 2, 1973**

'Sorry, I thought you said: "A thousand words are worth a picture"'

What to do

Before leaping to create visuals, it is worth asking yourself if you need them at all for this talk. Many outstanding talks have no visuals.

> **TIP**
>
> Use visuals only where they add value – not to accompany everything you say.

Choose or create powerful visuals in the form of:

- video clips;
- photographs;
- sketching an idea;

- animations;
- objects;
- equipment;
- diagrams;
- charts;
- maps;
- demonstrations.

Use your visuals to:

1 **Start or finish – or both**

   Since people easily recall what is first and last, it is a great place to show a vivid visual. Make that visual all about the core message you want people to remember.

2 **Create emotional appeal**

   Use vivid pictures of people, places, events, machines and so on to create feelings that will help your message, for example pictures that convey sadness, excitement, curiosity, delight or shock.

3 **Explain data**

   Show visuals such as graphs or charts that help to make data easier to understand. Check that the visual is easily understood and has impact.

4 **Make processes clear**

   A process gets fixed in the brain when we see it as a picture, for example, a linear process or cycle. Colour coding different parts in a process can make it easier to follow.

5 **Show relationships between elements**

   Show how parts relate to the whole, using visuals such as a family tree or an organisational chart. Have one visual for the whole, and then others that zoom in on each section.

6 Map out a topic

Use mind maps where ideas branch out from a central point. You can use them for numerous purposes such as scoping out a project or learning a topic. You will find guidance from Tony Buzan in his many books on the topic.

7 Bring the abstract to life

Abstract concepts, theories or models can be brought to life by creating colourful representations. A good example is showing a hierarchy of ideas as a pyramid shape.

8 Show a metaphor that makes your point

Create a powerful visual that conveys your point metaphorically: our project is like a military operation or we are like a motor-racing team.

See Secret 22 for help with slide design.

Your turn

1   Take an existing set of slides, if you have one, and check which visuals are really adding value. Remove or amend any that you consider weak, especially those that are mostly words rather than visual.

2   Look at your plan for an upcoming talk. Make a note of where visuals would help emphasise a message. Use Secret 22 as your guide when you create them.

Resource for further learning

Presentation Zen: Simple Ideas on Presentation Design and Delivery (2007) by Garr Reynolds.

Chapters 5, 6 and 7 give practical help on achieving simplicity in the design of slides.

Secret 22: Five rules to create memorable slides

The term 'death by PowerPoint' has become synonymous with boring presentations. Yet slides can actually be helpful when they are created with thoughtful attention to helping the audience.

In this Secret, we look at how to ensure that your slides add impact to your talk.

Why it matters

Poorly designed slides will:

● be more challenging for you to explain;

● make it harder for the audience to understand your points;

● often make your audience become tired;

People can't read and listen at the same time, yet they are asked to do just that in many presentations

- result in your talk being less enjoyable and less effective;

- decrease the chances of achieving your outcome.

What to do

Remember, your slides are there to help the audience reach your desired outcome.

Therefore, before you create a slide, ask:

- What is its purpose?

- Will this help the audience?

- Could I explain this better without a slide?

Once you have decided to create some slides, here is how:

Follow *all five* recommendations below to ensure that your slides help the audience's understanding.

1 Separate slides from handouts

People often use slides as handout documents.

When people attempt to create a slide that will also act as a handout, usually you have what Garr Reynolds refers to as a 'slide-u-ment'. It 'falls between two stools' as it does neither job well.

This is because a slide that is easy to grasp when explained by a speaker often contains too little information to be fully understood on its own. Likewise, a well-created handout document will be difficult to see on a screen.

As a rule: Great slides make poor handouts and great handouts make poor slides.

2 One message or idea per slide

Putting too many messages on one slide dilutes impact. Go for one message or idea per slide, even if that means you end up with more slides than you anticipated. It is better to have more slides than cramming too much on each one.

Keep slides separate from any handout documents you may give out to the audience

TIP

Do not give out a handout unless you want people to look at it there and then, because they will.

3 Use minimal words

Research from the University of New South Wales found that we cannot read and listen at the same time. Yet that is what happens as people try to read words on a screen while a presenter is speaking. It is mentally draining.

A single word or key message across the screen works because it can be read in seconds and can remain visible as the speaker elaborates.

Contrary to what most people think, the more text you have on your slides, the less your audience will remember.

Gavin Meikle, author of *The Presenter's Edge*

Meikle cites research by Dr Richard E. Meyer, published in *Multimedia Learning,* which found that the removal of bullet points produced a 28 per cent increase in the recall of information.

4 Turn information into pictures

● Turn numbers and data into diagrams or graphs.

● Use colour to increase memorability.

● Use strong contrasts to make words and images stand out.

● Show powerful photographs that ignite emotions in the audience.

● Show pictures of metaphors to convey ideas.

We have a mountain to climb

5 Include only what is needed

Avoid slides with 'visual clutter'. Get rid of everything on a slide except the elements that get your message across.

Graphs often have extra elements such as calibration marks, notes and even numbers that may not be needed to illustrate a trend. Take these elements off the slide.

One big picture will have more impact than several smaller ones. Leave space on a slide as helps make your information clearer.

Make it visual and make it memorable.

Your turn

1 Show the five recommendations to a colleague or friend.

2 Ask them to check your presentation slides to see how well you have done.

3 Listen to their feedback and make any adjustments.

Resource for further learning

Presentation Zen: Simple Ideas on Presentation Design and Delivery (2007) by Garr Reynolds.

An in-depth resource to help you create great slides.

Secret 23: Sketch your idea and make it stick

A quick sketch will get your ideas across instantly. All you need to draw are very simple pictures that convey meaning. If you can draw lines and shapes, then you can do it.

Why it matters

There is immense power in this informal way of presenting:

– It's immediate - when you draw a line you grab attention

– A very simple sketch will get an idea across

– Even a rough sketch stays in the memory so your drawing skill level need not be high

– A sketch helps people to follow your train of thought

– They literally see what you mean

– People love seeing a picture emerge

– It's different - a refreshing change from PowerPoint

When Spike sketches his proposal, they can literally see what he means

Drawing your idea 'live' is possibly the biggest trick to make it memorable.

What to do

1   Draw faces – they can be used in all kinds of topics

If you think you cannot draw, try drawing my character Spike below. It's a simple sequence.

Once you can draw Spike, you can create other characters using the same sequence.

All these faces are just variations of Spike. Have a go at drawing them.

2 Draw simple symbols to convey meaning

Now draw these shapes.

Next draw the pictures below, which are based on some of the shapes you just drew.

These pictures can have meanings – so they can symbolise ideas you want to convey:

Growth	Travel	Adventure
Solid	School	Vision
Nature	Transport	Goal

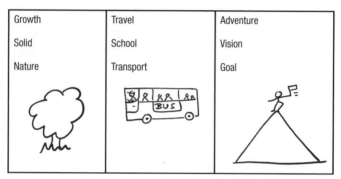

TIP

Use the same picture on lots of occasions because one symbol can mean many things.

Explain a vision with a picture

Sketch a metaphor to explain a project

3 Applications – here are examples of how you can apply these skills

When you combine symbols and add more information with lines, arrows and words, you can explain so much. People get it straight away when you turn ideas into pictures.

Here are some examples:

4 Choose from three approaches

(a) Start with a blank whiteboard or flipchart and draw it 'live' – 'on the fly'

Rather than have all the information pre-prepared, there is a captivating effect when people see a diagram or chart emerge before their eyes.

It is amazing how effortlessly people absorb a lot of information when presented in this way.

(b) Draw some of it in advance – and add the rest 'live'

You could have parts already done. This might save time, yet also give you the chance to hook in people by doing the rest 'live'.

Draw a flowchart to explain a process

(c) Draw it all in advance

This has less impact compared with drawing 'live'. However, it is a way of starting to introduce sketching until you feel confident to draw in front of a group. My tip is to move onto 'live' drawing at the earliest opportunity. Remember, drawings do not have to be perfect to convey your message.

Practise drawing skills and you will soon develop your technique.

For more tips on presenting using flipcharts and whiteboards, see the next Secret.

Your turn

Learn to draw your ideas. You need a pencil and paper and access to the following online talks by myself, which you will find on YouTube and www.ted.com.

● 'Why people believe they can't draw – and how to prove they can' TEDxHull.

● 'How to draw to remember more' TEDx Vienna.

1 Draw along with me as you watch these talks.

2 Choose one item from your next presentation that a sketch would help to explain.

3 Draw a rough draft of how you will do this, and then refine it ready for your talk.

Resource for further learning

The Art of Business Communication: How to use pictures, charts and graphics to make your message stick! (2014) by Graham Shaw.

Learn to sketch and present business ideas.

Secret 24: Six ways to add impact with flipcharts and whiteboards

Writing and sketching on a flipchart or whiteboard has amazing potential to make your message stick. Yet this approach often is ignored, perhaps because people are afraid of trying or underestimate just how easy and effective it can be.

Why it matters

As well as the reasons given in the previous Secret, the following are key:

– It's low tech, high impact - no need to spend time preparing slides

– It's an informal yet powerful way of presenting

– It's flexible - you can create ideas and amend them as you go along

– Using the tips below and techniques in Secret 23, you can make your ideas memorable

Flipcharts or whiteboards are in many offices and the ability to jump up and use them to explain your ideas is a skill worth developing.

What to do

Practical tips to help you get started:

1   Start with a blank page – the 'magic' way to get people hooked

Rather than have all the information pre-prepared, there is a captivating effect when people see a diagram or chart emerge before their eyes. It is amazing how much they can take in and how easy it is to follow when it is presented in this way.

2   Draw shapes, lines, arrows and symbols, to make ideas stick

Just like the cartoon at the start of this Secret, even with a few lines, arrows and shapes you can explain so much.

Turn your information into a visual such as a process, diagram or map.

If you think you cannot draw, see the previous secret where you can learn how easy it can be.

Karen was amazed how, even with her quite modest drawing, she was able to captivate the team

When Jeff started business updates with a blank whiteboard, he always got them hooked

TIP

Just have a go – it does not have to be a perfect sketch to be memorable.

---

3 Use lower-case writing – except for headings

Words written in capitals are always rectangular in their overall shape. This makes it harder to read the words quickly. Lower case is easier to read because each word has its own unique overall shape.

If you are writing a lot of words on a flipchart or whiteboard, write in lower-case letters

4 Use colours – they will make your message memorable

The brain loves colours because they are so memorable.

Make sure you have got a minimum of four colours to use – more if possible.

5 Use good quality pens

The main choices are chisel-tipped and bullet-tipped pens.

With a bullet tip you just get a thin line.

With chisel tipped you can get a thick or thin line, so these are my preference.

Do not rely on the venue having decent pens. Using poor quality or almost empty pens can hamper your talk.

Make sure you have good quality pens of your own available.

6 Stand to the side as you write or draw

Do not:

● stand where you are blocking any of the audience's view;

● turn your back on the audience.

Instead: stand so you can make eye contact with people, as shown in the cartoon of Karen explaining the customer journey earlier in this Secret.

Do:

● stand side-on to the flipchart or whiteboard;

● if you are right-handed, stand to the left of the flipchart;

● if you are left-handed, stand to the right;

● make sure people can see what you are writing or drawing all the time;

● when you are not actually writing, stand face-on where you can see everyone, and they can see the board.

Put the six tips into practice and have a go – make your presentation different.

Your turn

Develop your skills for presenting ideas on a flipchart or whiteboard. You need a pencil and a piece of paper.

1 Watch 'Draw Your Future' by Patti Dobrowolski, TEDxRainier (10-minute video). This is a great example of using simple sketches to present an idea.

2 Create a rough sketch of your own using Patti's template. It could be a different topic.

3 Review your sketch, refine it and then draw a finished version.

Resource for further learning

Visual Meetings: How Graphics, Sticky Notes & Idea Mapping Can Transform Productivity (2010) by David Sibbet.

See Chapter 5 'Presentation Without PowerPoint' for creative ways to communicate visually.

4

Add a little sparkle and drama

Secret 25: Four ways to grab attention in the first 30 seconds

An 'attention-grabber' instantly gets people engaged and, by relating it strongly to your message, you can maximise its impact.

Why it matters

- What you do first greatly influences audience perception.

- People remember what is first.

- People remember what is different.

- Attention-grabbers create mental states such as excitement, concern and astonishment.

- They can make powerful links into your topic.

  Just grabbing attention is not enough; you must link it to your message.

What to do

Here are four excellent attention-grabbers:

1   Give them an intriguing fact or startling statistics

Make people sit up and listen.

Jeremy grabbed attention with his magic umbrella trick, but the team were left wondering what it had to do with the business plan

Use one amazing fact or statistic.

Here is the start from David Epstein's talk at TED2014:

The runner of the 2012 Olympic marathon ran two hours and eight minutes. Had he been racing against the winner of the 1904 Olympic marathon, he would have won by nearly an hour and a half.

TIP

Make your fact a jaw-dropper.

Use a sequence of related facts or statistics.

Susan Pinkner, at TED2017, used two intriguing facts plus the promise of a third.

● *Here's an intriguing fact. In the developed world everywhere, women live an average of six to eight years longer than men do.*

- *In 2015, The Lancet published an article showing that men in rich countries are twice as likely to die as women are at any age.*

- *But there's one place in the world where men live as long as women.*

A sequence enables you to grab attention, then further build interest.

2   Use a prop

You might choose:

- an item of equipment;

- to demonstrate something using a prop, maybe a technique or a process;

- to pass an item around, such as a sample of the new product.

Ed Boyden used a baby's nappy, or diaper, at TEDSummit 2016.

He picked up the diaper and explained that the material that they are made from can swell up to 1,000 times in volume.

He then made a link to brain research. He wondered if he could use the same material that is in the diaper to make a brain swell up. If this material could swell as much in the brain as it does in the diaper, then it would enlarge the brain and make it easier to see.

The prop not only grabs attention but is memorable.

3   Make a bold claim

My claim, at TEDxHull, that I could teach the audience to draw cartoons, grabbed their attention. This was because, as mentioned in Secret 13, most people in the audience did not think they could draw.

The way you make a claim makes a difference:

- 'There is one thing that will make you more influential.'

- 'This memory technique will transform your ability to learn.'

- 'You can boost your fitness level in just 10 minutes a day.'

In your talks, think about what you could claim at the start that would really grab attention. It does not have to be over-dramatic, but must be something of value to the audience.

Phrase your claim in a compelling way.

4 Tell a story

The first line can really hook people:

- 'Last year I had an experience that changed my life . . .'

- 'One day I woke up with a great idea . . .'

- 'My daughter started ballet when she was four years old . . .'

Even though people do not know how the story relates to your talk, they will go with it. They know its purpose will be revealed.

Your turn

Create your own attention-grabber for an upcoming talk:

1 Write down three ideas to grab attention that you could relate to your talk.

2 Choose the one you feel is best.

3 Plan how you will introduce it.

Resource for further learning

'Underwater astonishments' by David Gallo at TED2007 (five-minute video). A great example of grabbing attention from the start.

Secret 26: Deliver a 'wow' moment they will remember forever

We have all experienced 'wow' moments when we have witnessed something amazing. When you create such a moment in your talk, and link it to your message, it is a powerful way to convince people.

Why it matters

Getting people to accept new ideas often requires their beliefs to be challenged. A 'wow' moment triggers an *emotionally charged response*.

The power of such moments can challenge the audience's beliefs much more effectively than trying to explain your point.

> *You're more likely to remember events that arouse your emotions than events that elicit a neutral response.*

Carmine Gallo, author of 'Talk Like TED'.

Your 'wow' moment could:

- make your audience laugh or cry;

- shake your audience's beliefs;

- cause your audience to see things differently;

- help your audience to remember your important message;

- prompt your audience to take action.

What to do

Create a moment that stands out from everything else.

Hedwig von Restorff, a psychiatrist and paediatrician, found that when one thing *differs* from the rest it is likely to be remembered. This is now known as

By popular demand, Michelle repeated her 'wow' moment 15 times, by which time they had all forgotten about the business update

the *isolation effect* or *von Restorff effect*. Notice which of the following words stands out: car, bus, train, bicycle, giraffe, lorry, aeroplane, ship.

Here are some ways to create your own 'wow' moment:

1 Give an experience that defies belief

A great example comes from the research entitled 'Gorilla in Our Midst' by Daniel J. Simons and Christopher F. Chabris (Harvard University, 1999).

Subjects were asked to watch a video of a group of people passing a basketball and count the number of passes. They were next asked if they had noticed the gorilla. Most people had not, even though a person in a gorilla suit had clearly wandered among the group. This demonstrates that often we see only what we are looking for, a phenomenon known as 'inattentional blindness' and this can be linked to many topics such as prejudice.

2 Get them to surprise themselves

Most people would be pleasantly surprised if they could draw someone we would all recognise.

Follow the sequence on the previous page to draw Einstein for yourself.

Drawing Einstein demonstrates that we all have untapped talents, which is just one of the learning points we might take from the exercise.

Other activities, such as impressive memory techniques, can create the same effect. You can learn impressive memory techniques from authors like Dominic O'Brien, eight times world memory champion.

3 Entertain them with a visual illusion

A visual illusion can be linked to so many messages.

A Fun Magic Colouring Book trick involves a children's colouring book of that name. As the audience watch you flick through, they see empty white pages. Flick again and all pages have black and white pictures. Flick yet again and the pages have coloured pictures. It's simple to perform, yet has people amazed. I have used it when working with children and linked the trick to the 'magic' of memory techniques.

You can relate the same trick to many different messages by changing the 'story' that you tell as you do the trick.

TIP

If you are stuck trying to think of a new 'wow' moment, use an existing one. Then find a way to link it back to your message.

Your turn

1 Write your talk's key message and think of a 'wow' moment you can link to it.

2 Work out how to use the Einstein drawing as a 'wow' moment in one of your talks.

3 Think of a way you can use *A Fun Magic Colouring Book.* You can find it at online booksellers.

Resource for further learning

Talk Like TED: The 9 Public Speaking Secrets of the World's Top Minds (2017) by Carmine Gallo.

Chapter 5 features guidance on creating 'jaw-dropping' moments.

Secret 27: Captivate your audience with stories and metaphors

A story or metaphor can get your idea across instantly because people just love them. They have the power to evoke emotions that help you appeal to the heart.

Why it matters

> *Many cognitive scientists now conclude that people not only talk in metaphor, but also think and reason in metaphor.*
>
> James Lawley and Penny Tompkins, authors of *Metaphors in Mind*

'In a metaphor, information seems to come ready-packed in a way that makes it easy to pass on,' write Wendy Sullivan and Judy Rees, authors of *Clean Language*. This metaphor from Oscar Wilde exemplifies their point: 'Memory is the diary that we all carry about with us.'

Speaking metaphorically is so natural that people do it without realising. Phrases such as, 'We're skating on thin ice' or 'This is the thin end of the wedge' are common.

Using stories and metaphors enables you to:

- connect emotionally;
- trigger the imagination;
- create curiosity because people want to know what happens next;
- help people remember your talk;
- get a message over without it sounding like a lecture;

- help people to effortlessly absorb information;

- bypass conscious resistance to new ideas.

What to do

Here are some great choices:

1 Start with a story

'A mountain not far from here was the scene of the most remarkable occurrence . . .' Starting with a story gets them hooked. Generally, just go straight in without explanation to create maximum impact.

2 'It happened to me . . .' tell *your* story

A personal story is a great way to connect with a group:

'Just yesterday I was paying for my shopping when I was struck by a thought . . .'

Telling a true story adds a powerful personal dimension.

The team could see Gloria's point, but thought she may have taken the metaphor too far

3   Tell someone else's story

'I'd like to tell you about a girl called Ellie who wanted to be a dancer, but there was just one problem . . .' You can tell their story in ways that you just could not if it was about yourself. You can speak objectively about their character, talents and virtues in ways that would seem immodest if it was about you.

4   Prove your point with a story

Until Roger Bannister broke the four-minute mile, many thought it impossible. However, proving it could be done convinced others that they could do it too. Just 46 days later, it was broken again and a year later three athletes broke 4 minutes in a *single race*. Always look for a story that will back up your point.

5   Use metaphor to turn abstract into concrete

Ideas are easier to understand if we make them concrete. In their book *Made to Stick,* Chip and Dan Heath explain why, by using a *simile,* which works like metaphor because it helps us grasp how one thing is *like* another: 'Trying to teach an abstract principle without concrete foundations is like trying to start a house by building a roof in the air.'

6   Back up logical evidence with a story

Aristotle emphasised the need for emotional connection instead of just giving facts. Therefore, back up your data with a story. For example, medical data could be backed up with a true story about the success of a treatment.

7   End with a story

Create a memorable ending with a story that encapsulates your key message.

Include story and metaphor in every talk and you will soon be well-practised.

Your turn

1   Next time you explain something in conversation try saying: '*It's rather like . . . .*'

2   Identify a metaphor that will help people understand an idea in one of your talks.

3   Choose a story or anecdote that will support a key point in your talks.

Resource for further learning

The Storyteller's Secret: How TED Speakers and Inspirational Leaders Turn Their Passion into Performance (2018) by Carmine Gallo.

Very helpful if you want to learn how telling powerful stories can inspire and change lives.

Secret 28: How to use humour in a talk

Many talks can benefit from humour and lightness but there is the potential to get it wrong. We have all heard remarks that were intended to be funny but 'went down like a lead balloon'.

Why it matters

Well-used humour can:

● build rapport and lift the mood of the audience;

● make a talk entertaining;

● make key messages memorable.

What to do

1 Use observational humour

The funniest remarks are often not jokes at all, but simply observations to which the audience can relate. It is like holding up a mirror to life. Not only does it raise a laugh, but also it demonstrates that you have something in common with the audience.

- 'Why is it that, when you are in a rush, the queue seems to move so slowly?'

- 'Have you ever gone into a room and forgotten why you went in there?'

- 'Is it just me? Or do you find that, whenever you enquire about these low-priced offers, none of them is available?'

These are not funny in themselves. However, they may cause a smile because people can relate to them.

Sadly, his favourite joke didn't hit the mark, but Gerald thought they were bound to love hearing about his hilarious camping holiday

2 Tell jokes that enhance your message

A joke out of the blue will cause the audience to wonder what is going on. Therefore, the way you lead into a joke is important. If the joke relates to your message, then the audience will see its relevance.

TIP

Make a strong link into a joke so the point of telling it is obvious.

Phrases that help you lead into a joke:

- 'The problem we have is very much like the person who was trying to . . .'

- 'It's rather like the man who asked the doctor for a . . .'

- 'Managing this project reminds me of the man who was attempting to . . .'

Avoid humour that may cause even the slightest offence.

3 Use anecdotes relevant to your topic

Anecdotes can be amusing without giving the appearance of joke-telling.

Many would agree that real life is more amusing than fictional humour. A well-chosen anecdote can both illustrate your point and add humour.

4 Learn from others but develop your own style

We can learn a lot from professional comedians and many of their techniques can be incorporated into talks. However, there are vast differences between a stage show and events such as business or educational presentations. Expectations are entirely different. Therefore, we need to keep this in mind when we use humour.

5 Be on the alert for naturally occurring opportunities for humour

Humour can arise naturally and often unexpectedly in talks. It may be a comment from an audience member. It could be something you say yourself in response to a comment or question. Be ready to embrace and build on humour when it occurs naturally.

Your turn

1 If you are not used to telling jokes, why not practise among good friends.

2 Think of an appropriate and amusing anecdote to make a point in your next talk.

3 Next time you see an amusing speaker, identify one thing that you could emulate.

Resource for further learning

'Do schools kill creativity?' by Sir Ken Robinson, TED2006 (19-minute video).

Great example of using humour in a talk.

Part 2

Practising

5

It is OK to be nervous

Secret 29: You do not need to be totally Zen to get through it

We all want to feel calm when on stage and, though calmness is a useful state, a small dose of nerves can help your performance.

Why it matters

Being *too* relaxed can lead to complacency.

In sport, there are countless examples where the underdog beats the favourite. Strong favourites often cannot escape the mindset that they are bound to win.

By contrast, underdogs often psych themselves up into a high-performance state. Their focus and concentration is at its best and they are 'ready to go.'

In speaking it is the same – you must be 'on your game' to be outstanding.

- If you are too relaxed, you can become careless.
- With sharp mental focus, you will speak better.
- When you feel confident, but not over-confident, you are likely to perform well.
- Only when you are 'up for it' can you perform at the top of your game.

Tom was so engrossed in pumping himself up for the weekly update that he hadn't noticed the team had already arrived

If a speaker had no nerves, I would question how much their talk mattered.

What to do

The following will help you to get into a high-performance state:

1 Act *as if* you are confident

When you pretend to be powerful, you are more likely to actually feel powerful.

Amy Cuddy, speaking at TEDGlobal 2012 about research at Harvard University

Research subjects were asked to hold poses for two minutes each. The first involved closed and hunched 'low-power' postures. The second were all 'high-power' postures, such as standing upright, feet planted apart and hands on hips.

After two minutes in high-power poses, tests showed marked increases in testosterone, the dominance hormone. This was accompanied by significant decreases in cortisol, the stress hormone. The opposite was true for those who adopted low-power poses. Therefore, spending two minutes before a talk standing in a powerful way can help you to feel more powerful and confident.

2 Identify what has got you into a high-performance state in other situations

Use what has worked for you before. Perhaps listening to certain music boosts your mood. Maybe what you wear affects your confidence. In these examples, music and clothes can be what are known as 'anchors'. 'An anchor is a stimulus, it may be a sound, an image, touch, smell or taste, that triggers a consistent response in you or others,' says Knight, author of *NLP at Work*. Think about the anchors that will work for you.

3 Create your routines for use in future talks

Actors often follow the same routine before a performance. Routines are useful ways to repeatedly access high-performance states. Think about the build-up to your talk and what will work for you, such as arriving early.

We are all different – notice what works for you.

4 Prepare your talk in the way that makes you feel comfortable

Everyone is different in how they need to prepare. You will know what kind of preparation you have to do to feel comfortable. Be guided by your intuition. You just know when something is not right – have the courage to change it.

5 Visualise success

Once your talk is ready, go through it in your mind. See it as if you are really there. Notice the detail of what you see and hear. Visualise in the positive, i.e. what you *want*, not what you do not want. Like an athlete imagining a perfect performance, you are increasing the chances of it happening.

Your turn

Create your own high-performance state:

1 Write down three things that help you feel positive, uplifted or confident. Maybe listening to a song, wearing a suit or picturing a past success in your mind.

2 Tick any of these that you could use in future to feel positive about a talk.

3 Write your ideal routine to go through before you speak.

Resource for further learning

'Your body language may shape who you are', Amy Cuddy, TEDGlobal 2012 (21-minute video).

Secret 30: Calm your nerves with a breath . . . and more

When we are anxious, our attention is not in the present. Most often, that is because we are worrying about what *has* happened or what *might* happen. This is sometimes described as being 'off-centre' as opposed to feeling 'centred.' Our stress hormone, cortisol, increases and we are inhibited from performing well.

Just take a deep breath to bring you back to the present moment.

Why it matters

To give our best performance we need to be fully *present*.

When you are anxious and not fully present:

● you cannot think clearly;

● it can lead to nausea, headaches and more;

● you tend adopt behaviours showing that you are nervous;

- the audience has less confidence in you;
- you may go into flight or fight mode or freeze like a rabbit in the headlights;
- you may become fearful, which impairs good performance.

Although Rachael hated public speaking, she couldn't wish for a more supportive team

What to do

Three easy things to do when you start feeling anxious:

1 Breathe deeply to re-centre yourself

Guidance based upon the work of Wendy Palmer and Janet Crawford in 'Leadership Embodiment' suggests we breathe in deeply as if breathing upwards. Then breathe out in a long breath as if exhaling down the front of our body. Maintain an upright stance throughout. Imagine you have soft shoulders and relax them. Even after several breaths, you can feel a difference as your attention is brought back to the present moment.

The way we sit and stand can change the way we think and speak.

Wendy Palmer and Janet Crawford, authors of *Leadership Embodiment*

2 Reframe anxious experiences to a positive

When we give negative meanings to things that happen it makes us feel anxious. However, we can choose to *positively reframe* those experiences. All we need to do is ask ourselves: 'What else it could mean?'

Here are a couple of examples:

Having made a mistake at the start of a talk, your instinctive reaction might be:

● 'I've made a mistake, so this is going to be awful.'

Taking a moment to positively reframe the experience, you might more helpfully think:

● 'That's an early sign to keep me on my toes.'

After forgetting where you were in your talk, your instinctive reaction might be:

● 'There you go – typical me!'

Taking a moment to positively reframe the experience, you might more helpfully think:

● 'Anyone can forget something. I'll make sure I find a way to avoid that happening next time.'

TIP

Drink water because dehydration causes stress – and stress causes dehydration. 'Studies have shown that being just half a litre dehydrated can increase your cortisol levels,' according to Amanda Carlson, performance nutritionist.

---

3 Place a positive label on the 'negative' feeling

Feelings that we typically label positive or negative are often similar feelings.

'Nervous' often feels like 'excited'.

A quick way to overcome nerves is to change the label we give them. Instead of saying: 'I feel nervous' or 'I've got butterflies', we could, instead, say: 'I feel a sense of anticipation' or 'That's excitement.'

Remember to change the label you give to a negative feeling in order to change your reaction into a positive.

Your turn

1 Next time you become aware that you are getting anxious or impatient, for example in a queue, practise the breathing exercise described above to re-centre and ground yourself.

2 Practise reframing your own reactions; notice when you next react negatively to something. Remind yourself that you have simply labelled it as bad. Now think of a positive meaning for it.

Resource for further learning

Leadership Embodiment – How the Way We Sit and Stand Can Change the Way We Think and Speak (2013) by Wendy Palmer and Janet Crawford.

Chapter 5 has a range of techniques that can help when you feel pressured. The book helps the reader to develop personal power and presence through mindfulness and the body.

Secret 31: You do not have to be word-perfect, but it can help

How do I remember what to say? The thought of going blank can cause great anxiety.

There is not just one solution, but here are examples of best practice to help you choose what will be most effective for you.

Why it matters

Knowing what works best for you will enable you to:

- prepare in ways that help you feel comfortable;
- be flexible in your approach to preparation to fit the demands of different talks;
- optimise your preparation and rehearsal time;
- remember everything you want to say;
- give the best performance possible.

Learning his lines wasn't a problem for Tim; recalling them was the issue

When you are on the stage is not the time to be creating your talk.

What to do

Look at the three methods below and decide what works best for you.

You might choose different approaches for different talks.

1 Script the talk and memorise it

Pros

- You say exactly what you want to say.

- You avoid saying things that with forethought could have been said better.

- You learn the content really well so you can focus on *how* to deliver it.

- It helps you stick to time constraints.

Cons

- It often takes a lot of time and effort to memorise it.

TIP

Record your script and play it back to help you learn it.

When you might choose this method

- If the talk is 'high-stakes' and everything must be spot on.

- If the talk is short enough to memorise; for most people 15 minutes is do-able.

- If your instinct tells you that you *must* use this method to feel comfortable.

2 Write bullet points for the talk – but script key lines to memorise

Pros

- It Is quicker than learning a whole script.

- You can still ensure that key lines are memorised.

- You are still thoroughly prepared content-wise.

Cons

- It still requires learning of key lines, which may take time.

When you might choose this method

- When time does not allow you to memorise a script.

- If it is not vital to say the exact wording for most of it.

- When the key lines are best said verbatim to maximise impact.

3 Just write bullet points

In this approach, you create bullet point notes to guide what you say.

Pros

- You talk naturally about each point.

- It is quicker than having to learn a script.

- You avoid the potential anxiety of trying to recall exact words.

- If you rehearse enough, it helps you memorise without trying.

Chris Anderson, Head of TED, in his book *TED Talks,* quotes Mary Roach as having no script but preparing note cards instead. She says: 'There's a kind of unintentional memorising that develops from repetition.'

Cons

- You may say things that, with hindsight, could have been better phrased.

- Bullet points do not specify the finer detail of what you want to say, so it is just possible that you might forget to say something.

When you might choose this method

- When you feel that learning a script is not practical or necessary.

- If you feel more comfortable not trying to remember a script.

- Unless you are regularly giving high-stakes talks where you feel the need to memorise a script, bullet points will suffice most of the time.

- For lower-stakes talks such as team meetings or possibly client meetings.

- For high-stakes talks *providing you are prepared to rehearse* many times.

Decide what works best for you.

What do I do if I forget what I was going to say next?

Remember:

- It happens to many speakers and it is not the end of the world.

- A short silence is fine.

- People do not know what you were going to say next anyway.

Take steps to reduce the chances of forgetting:

- If you worry about going blank, it might be best *not* to memorise word-for-word.

- Have key points on cue cards nearby. Just knowing they are available can reduce anxiety.

Plan what to do if you do forget:

- Take a deep breath.

- Have a drink of water.

- If you still cannot recall what you were going to say . . .

- Look at your cue cards and find where you were.

- Resume your talk.

When you find your preferred method, use it consistently to make life easier.

Your turn

Try this quick exercise to improve your ability to remember your talk:

1 Write down what you currently do to remember what to say.

2 Highlight what works well and what does not.

3 Write down three things to do differently next time.

Resource for further learning

TED Talks: The Official TED Guide to Public Speaking (2018) by Chris Anderson, Head of TED.

Chapter 11 'Scripting' contains plenty of practical guidance on this aspect.

The chapter includes many examples of how TED speakers remember what to say.

Secret 32: Have a walk-through 'in your head' to spot problems

For my TEDxHull talk, I had the idea of placing a packet of drawing pens under every seat. However, as part of my preparation, I did a 'walk-through' in my head and realised that the audience could not open the packets quickly or quietly. I felt that to start like this would seem rather disorganised and cause delay. To make it easier on the day itself, I had the back of the packets removed. It worked; the audience could instantly get at the pens. That walk-through in my head helped me anticipate a problem and imagine a solution.

Sandra had already visualised the microphone packing up so was well prepared when it did

Imagining what might go wrong is useful.

Why this matters

Everything counts and a 'walk-through' in your head enables you to:

- check your talk at various stages of preparation;
- imagine how ideas might or might not work;
- get a feel for how it is coming along;
- become aware of issues that could cause problems for you;
- imagine yourself coping with those problems;
- ditch some ideas and introduce better ones;
- feel confident when you have checked everything in detail.

What to do

In a study published in the *Journal of Experimental Social Psychology* (July 2011), Heather Kappes and Gabriele Oettingen suggest '*critical visualisation*'. This means imagining potential obstacles and things that might go wrong. When we imagine such obstacles, we are motivated to overcome them. Once we see ourselves coping with such problems in our mind, it gives us more confidence that we can do it.

Use the steps below to have a walk-through in your head to spot problems.

1   Gather all the information you can about the situation

- The room layout.
- How people are seated.
- Positioning of equipment.
- Where you will stand.
- Potential problems.

2   Find a quiet place and imagine you are there in the room

- It may help to close your eyes.
- See the detail through *your own* eyes.

- Make it as real as you can.
- Be aware of what you hear.
- How does it feel?
- What else are aware of?

TIP

The deeper you can immerse yourself in the experience, the more you will notice.

---

3 Walk through your talk

- Start going through the talk in your mind.
- Look out to the audience.

As you go through the sequence of your talk notice:

- What is going well?
- Where does it feel great?
- Where does it feel uneasy?
- Where is there something missing?
- When there is a problem, notice how you cope with it.

4 Come out of the visualisation and write a list of what you learnt

- What went well?
- What went wrong or caused concern?
- How well did you cope in responding to problems?
- What was beyond your control?
- What will you do to address the problems identified?

Do repeated walk-throughs in your head to eliminate more problems.

Your turn

1 Think of a talk coming up and use the four steps described above to have a walk-through in your mind.

2 Imagine any problems and how you are coping with them.

3 Afterwards make a note of any issues to resolve.

Resource for further learning

'Tapping the Power of Mental Rehearsal' by Brett Steenbarger, 17 February 2018, Forbes, see: www.forbes.com/sites/brettsteenbarger/2018/02/17/tapping-the-power-of-mental-rehearsal/#70ac746766f0.

Secret 33: Rehearse, rehearse, rehearse

It sounds logical to *first* create a talk and *then* rehearse it. However, it is not always like that in practice. Best practice by successful speakers shows that there are often two types of rehearsal.

The first is what could be called the *creating rehearsal* in which you are *still creating content* while practising. This is an important, yet generally unnoticed, stage.

The second is what people normally think of as rehearsing. It might be described as a *polishing rehearsal* in which you practise the content you have *already created*.

Why it matters

Being aware of the two kinds of rehearsal will help you to decide how *you* should rehearse.

You need to rehearse in the right way for you because:

● everyone is different and what works for someone else may not work for you;

● it will optimise your preparation time;

- you will feel more comfortable and confident on the day;

- you are more likely to give your best possible performance.

Ken liked to talk 'off the top of his head' to develop his talk. When he listened back, there was always one gem of a phrase he could use

What to do

Read through the suggestions below for each type of rehearsal and decide what suits you.

The 'creating' rehearsal

Chris Anderson, in his book *TED Talks,* mentions Clay Shirky, who gave a talk at the TED offices without writing a script. Instead, he *created* the talk by rehearsing it.

Shirky says: 'I prepare for a talk by talking.' At the start, it is 'more editing than rehearsing'. Even once his talk is developed, he still does not script it, but instead makes notes.

Here are my recommendations for rehearsing in this way:

1 Have key bullets of your structure visible

- Have your notes on cards.

- Write bullets on a flipchart.

- Put sticky notes on your wall.

2   Stand and use gestures

- Standing up gets you into the presenting mode.

- As per the research described in Secret 48, when you use gestures it helps you find your words.

3   Capture the gems

- Have a friend or colleague there to make notes.

- Stop when you come out with a great line and write it down.

- Record on audio or video.

4   Review and refine before next practice

- Make a note of what worked and what did not.

- Refine content and/or structure.

- Modify your bullet point notes or script.

Once you have it well developed, do your 'polishing rehearsal' as described below.

TIP

Focus on practising and developing parts that give you most concern.

The 'polishing' rehearsal

The purpose of having a scripted talk is to help you memorise it word for word. In a bullet-pointed talk, the purpose is to ensure that you can find suitable words.

1   Give extra attention to less familiar parts

Kenny Werner (American jazz pianist, composer and author) recommends that, in learning music, instead of thinking of some parts as 'difficult', think of them as 'less familiar'. Use that positive mindset and, as those sections become familiar, they will be easier.

2 Memorise opening and closing lines

Even if you are not using a scripted talk, decide what you will say first and last. It will give you confidence for a great start and finish.

3 Learn the links between one thing and the next

Do this because links help you remember what is coming next.

4 Make it realistic

If possible, use the same equipment and set up as on the day and ask a few people to be the audience.

5 Get feedback

Do not rely on your own view. See Secret 34 for guidance on receiving feedback.

Mastery is playing whatever you are playing . . . every time. . . without thinking.

Kenny Werner, author of Effortless Mastery

Rehearsing well will enable you to give a masterful performance.

Your turn

Try this short exercise to get used to the 'creating rehearsal':

1 Identify a small section from a talk you have yet to fully think through.

2 Write bullet point content.

3 Set up an audio or video recording device such as a smartphone.

4 Start talking, being guided by the bullet points.

5 Review the recording and write down phrases that sounded good.

6 Incorporate those into your talk script or guide notes.

Resource for further learning

TED Talks: The Official TED Guide to Public Speaking by Chris Anderson, Head of TED.

Chapter 12 'Run-Throughs' includes wisdom from TED speakers on how to rehearse.

Secret 34: Find some guinea pigs for feedback

We never see ourselves as others do. If you rely just on your own opinion to check your presentation or talk, then you are guaranteed to miss important things. Good feedback is like gold dust and can improve your talk immensely.

Why it matters

Feedback enables you to:

- get a totally different perspective on your talk;
- gain insights that you would never have thought of;
- learn what is already working;
- find out what is not working;
- identify what to do to enhance your talk.

We all need people who will give us feedback. That's how we improve.

Bill Gates

What to do

1 Gather feedback on four areas

- Content – is the message clear?
- Structure – does the sequence and flow work?
- Visuals – do your slides have impact?
- Presentation style – are you displaying enough energy and is your voice and body language working well?

One piece of feedback could make the difference.

Beryl's practice was so realistic that her guinea pigs leapt at her call-to-action!

2 Decide who best to ask

Ask non-experts and experts.

● Experts are of obvious value.

● However, the opinion of people new to you and your subject is helpful, too.

In his book *TED Talks,* Chris Anderson, Head of TED, shares the experience of speaker Rachel Botsman.

To summarise, she admits it was a mistake to run through one of her talks only with people who already know her and her work. The best feedback, in her view, is from people: 'who can tell you where there are gaps in your narrative or where you are making assumptions'.

Practise your talk in front of someone who knows nothing about your work.

Rachel Botsman, Oxford University lecturer, author and TED speaker

Ask individuals and groups:

● An individual can give you in-depth feedback.

● A group can replicate an audience and offer you many views.

3 Ask for feedback at key stages

● Early – while developing ideas and before you get too fixed about your talk.

Ask especially for feedback on content and structure at this stage.

● Midway – before it is too late to change things.

Content and structure should be well-established, yet you still have time to alter it.

Ask for feedback on all four areas: content, structure, visuals and presentation style.

● Rehearsals near the day

These rehearsals are for practising a finished talk. A rehearsal very close to the day of the talk is not the time to receive major feedback, which may lead to rewriting sections. Unless something vital arises, you want to identify only minor refinements at this stage.

Ask especially for feedback on presentation style but be open to tweaks on content, structure and visuals.

● After the talk itself

Feedback at this time is especially valuable if your talk is to be repeated.

4 Ask for verbal and written feedback

Ask for both if possible to maximise the learning opportunity.

5 Ask for two kinds of feedback

Ask observers to structure their feedback into two sections:

● What worked well?

● What should I do differently?

TIP

Ask observers to be specific in their feedback.

We love to hear praise that says we are fantastic. However this is too general to be of real use. It does not tell us *what* we did well. Instead, ask for *evidence,* for example, what did they *see* and *hear*?

6 Guidelines for receiving feedback

● *Listen* – avoid justifying or being defensive.

● *Check your understanding* – ask questions to clarify, seek examples.

● *Compare views* – is the same view held by others?

● *Take a positive view* – the aim of feedback is to help you learn.

● *Acknowledge the giver* – show appreciation. Feedback is not always easy to give.

● *Make a choice* – you may wish to act on the feedback, or not.

Your turn

Improve your speaking skills, or a specific talk, by making a note of:

1 What would you most like feedback on?

2 Who is best to ask?

3 When will you ask them?

Resources for further learning

The following are to be found at the back of the book.

1 'Observing presentations – what to look for': this is a guide for your observers, which you may wish to reproduce to give each one a copy.

2 'Observer's feedback form': this is a suggested template that you could recreate and give out so that observers can write comments for you.

Part 3

Performing

6

What to say and how to say it

Secret 35: Make sure your words, voice and body language all say the same thing

Have you ever noticed that sometimes people say 'yes', but it sounds like they mean 'no'? Perhaps you have been in conversation with someone who claimed they were listening, but seemed more interested in something over your shoulder or out of the window? In these instances, we are receiving conflicting messages.

Why it matters

Communication involves three components:

- words;
- voice qualities such as tone, pitch, speed or volume;
- body language such as gestures, facial expression and posture.

> *For our communication to be effective all three of these must be in sync.*
>
> Emma Ledden, author of *The Presentation Book*

When they are not synchronised, the message is often ambiguous.

When we find a message ambiguous, we tend to rely on the voice and body language.

This means we take more meaning from voice and body language than the actual words, as we try to interpret what people are really saying and feeling. When someone says: 'I am listening, do carry on . . . ' while looking at their phone, it is not surprising that you might believe their actions more than their words.

'I'm so excited to see you all here today . . . '

What to do

Make sure your words, voice and body language match.

Be congruent in your words, voice and body language to build trust.

To send the audience one clear message:

1 Choose your words carefully

Prepare words and phrases that say exactly what you want. Different words evoke different feelings and are received differently. Notice how the following *similar phrases* all have slightly *different meanings:* 'How about this idea', 'I have a suggestion', 'Here's my recommendation' or 'You might like this useful tip'.

For more help on phrasing, see Secret 36.

2 Use the voice that conveys exactly what you mean

Even when attending to just the words and voice, we can hear how meaning can change depending on aspects such as voice, tone and emphasis.

Just emphasising a different word can change the whole meaning.

Say this phrase and emphasise the italicised word to hear how the meaning changes:

- 'I never said he *stole* that money.'

- 'I never said he stole *that* money.'

- 'I never said *he* stole that money.'

- 'I *never* said he stole that money.'

- 'I never *said* he stole that money.'

- '*I* never said he stole that money.'

- 'I never said he stole that *money.*'

Therefore, speak in a way that conveys exactly what you want to say. Speak with energy, passion and conviction when appropriate, otherwise your audience may receive a diluted version of your message. For more help on using your voice, see Secrets 39, 40 and 41.

3 Use the body language that backs up your message

Two speakers could say exactly the same words in a presentation, yet one could get the message across much better than the other because of body language.

Match body language to words and voice. For example, when you have assertive words to say, use a firm voice, serious facial expression and an upright body posture.

For more on how to use body language well, see Secrets 46, 47, 48, 49 and 50.

What to be careful of

Do not overthink it. Pay attention to voice and body language but remember to be yourself because it is not about being robotic.

TIP

Practise your talk and ask for feedback on how well your words, voice and body language match.

Your turn

Enhance your awareness of words, voice and body language.

In a meeting or social gathering:

1   Notice how body language gives signals about how people are feeling.

2   Look for sudden changes.

3   Notice how voice tone conveys feelings.

4   Identify when someone's voice and body language does or does not match their words.

Resource for further learning

The Definitive Book of Body Language: How to Read Others' Attitudes by Their Gestures (2017) by Allan and Barbara Pease.

For a detailed insight into body language for many kinds of communication.

Secret 36: How to speak simply so people get the message instantly

It is easy to use over-complicated language and people may even purposely use clever-sounding or 'sophisticated' words. David Oppenheimer reported: 'When 110 Stanford University undergraduates were polled about their writing habits, most of them admitted that they had made their writing more complex in order to appear smarter.' But does this use of more complex language achieve the desired effect?

Why it matters

Most presenters want to make it easy for the audience to understand them. They would also prefer their audience to be pleased with their choice of words.

What does the research say?

With regard to the 110 students mentioned above, Oppenheimer's research found that: 'Such strategies tend to backfire.'

He conducted experiments at Stanford to compare the effects of simple or complex written language. He concluded that the results strongly suggested that: 'Complex vocabulary makes texts harder to read, which in turn lowers judgements of the author's intelligence.'

Therefore, write as simply as possible.

What about the spoken word?

Expert advice for the spoken word also recommends simplicity. I watched a professional radio presenter transform a script for a senior manager's speech. He took out the big words and replaced them with simple language. The resulting speech was so much easier to follow.

Simpler words are easier to process and make you sound smarter

What to do

Do the five things below when writing notes, slides and handouts for your talks.

1   Use short simple words

Unless a longer word really does explain it better.

Derek was looking good, but no one knew what on earth he was talking about

2 Use short sentences

When people hear or read a long sentence, they have to hold a lot of information in their head as the sentence unfolds. You can spare them this challenge by being brief.

Adam Frankel was speech writer to Barack Obama and says that when preparing a speech you should: 'Write like you talk.' He suggests you: 'avoid awkward constructions' because they are more likely to cause you to stumble.

TIP

Read the speech aloud as you're writing. If you do it enough, you'll start hearing the words when you type them.

Adam Frankel, speech writer for Barack Obama

---

3   Use the 'active voice' phrasing

Active voice phrasing is where the *subject* of the sentence performs the action. This is as opposed to the *passive voice* phrasing where the subject is *acted upon* by the verb.

Got it? Possibly not, because it is easier to grasp with simple examples below:

● Do not use the *passive voice* by saying: 'The marketing plan was written by David.'

● Instead, use the *active voice* and say: 'David wrote the marketing plan.'

   Just put the subject (in this case 'David') at the start.

4   Leave out unnecessary words

● Omit words that do not add anything: 'Mary *carried out* research on market trends.'

● Reduce to: 'Mary researched market trends.'

● If you have a written script, go through it and remove unnecessary words.

5   Avoid jargon – use words everyone can understand

You may have been in presentations where you had not got a clue what some of the words and phrases meant: 'fashionise', 'financial footprint', 'run it up the flagpole', 'leverage our brand', 'zero cycles'. The list of jargon is endless, as is its capacity to alienate and irritate.

Use only words that your whole audience understands, which includes avoiding jargon. If you use specialist terminology then you need to explain it.

If you are speaking to an audience of specialists, then it may be different because you can use specialist terminology that everyone understands.

Your turn

1   Write a simpler word that could replace each of the following:

● Commence _____

● Subsequently _____

- Endeavour _____
- Proximity _____
- Promulgate _____

2 Choose a piece of your own writing, such as notes for a talk, slides or a document. Replace any complex words and phrases with simpler ones.

Resource for further learning

How to Write an Easy Read: Retrain Your Brain to Write Simply and Clearly With These 10 Lessons (2016) by Lynette Clarke.

Secret 37: Use rhetorical questions to get people on the edge of their seats

Why is it that, even when you think your topic is interesting, the audience can still seem hard-going? Wouldn't it be great if there was a way to get them really motivated to listen? Well there is because rhetorical questions can do just that.

Why it matters

- **You cannot assume interest**

  Many business presentations are compulsory. Even if people have some interest, it is up to the presenter to increase it.

- **You can build a sense of anticipation**

  When a rollercoaster slowly climbs a steep slope, it builds anticipation of the descent. You can increase anticipation of your talk with rhetorical questions.

- **Curiosity engages people and means they want to know more**

  When you start something but do not let people know how it finishes, you are opening a loop. Have you ever missed the end of a film and felt disappointed? You were disappointed because you remained curious. The loop closes only when you know how the film ends.

Pamela never failed to create curiosity with her rhetorical questions

Curiosity helps people learn in more ways than you think.

Research from the University of California found that when we are curious about a topic it helps us to remember it.

Perhaps, more surprisingly, researchers found that when participants were in a curious state they could also recall *unrelated information.*

Co-author of the study, Matthias Gruber, reported:

> *Curiosity may put the brain into a state that allows it to learn and retain any kind of information, like a vortex that sucks in what you are motivated to learn, and also everything around it.*

> *Curiosity about one thing helps people remember other things, too.*

What to do

1   Ask rhetorical questions to create curiosity

Rhetorical questions do not require answers, but they get people thinking, as in the examples from the following two talks.

- 'How great leaders inspire action' by Simon Sinek, TEDxPuget Sound, 2009.

His opening words are:

How do you explain when things don't go as we assume?

Or better, how do you explain when others are able to achieve things that seem to defy all of the assumptions?

For example, why is Apple so innovative?

He builds anticipation before revealing what he has discovered.

- 'What makes a good life? Lessons from the longest study on happiness' by Robert Waldinger, TEDxBeaconStreet, 2015.

He starts with:

What keeps us happy and healthy as we go through life? If you were going to invest now in your future best-self, where would you put your time and your energy?

He continues for around two minutes building up curiosity. Then he concludes his opening with two more rhetorical questions:

But – what if we could watch entire lives as they unfold through time? What if we could study people from the time that they were teenagers all the way into old age to see what keeps them happy and healthy?

By this time, the audience are hooked and motivated to hear what comes next.

2 Open your talk with a great phrase

- 'Have you ever wondered . . . ?'

- 'Has it occurred to you . . . ?'

- 'Wouldn't it be great if we could . . . '

- 'Why is it that every time . . . ?'

- 'Am I the only person who . . . ?'

- 'Have you noticed . . . ?'

- 'Is it just me or . . . ?'

- 'Have you experienced . . . ?'
- 'Wouldn't it be great if . . . ?'
- 'Why do people . . . ?'

Use rhetorical questions both at the start and during your talk.

Your turn

1 Think of a typical talk you might do or one that is coming up.

2 Write six rhetorical questions to create curiosity.

3 Practise the start of your talk, integrating several of your best questions.

Resource for further learning

'How great leaders inspire action', Simon Sinek, TEDxPugetSound Washington, (18-minute video).

Good example of using rhetorical questions.

Secret 38: Repeat it so they remember it, repeat it so they remember it

To achieve your outcomes, people need to remember the most important points. Repetition is one of the best ways to achieve this.

Why it matters

Repetition matters because:

- it makes it clear what is most important;
- repeating a message makes it familiar;
- research shows that a familiar idea is more likely to be accepted and trusted;
- when people accept and trust your ideas, it increases the chance of them taking action.

Mary thought that repeating her message would help, but the team seemed puzzled

Repetition is one of the most powerful variables affecting memory.

Douglas L. Hintzman on his laboratory research
'Psychology of Learning and Motivation', Vol. 10, 1976

What to do

1 Decide what is worth repeating

Ask: what do the audience need to remember to achieve the outcome?

Typically, this might well be your core message or three key ideas.

TIP

Repeat the most important message that you want them to take away.

---

2 Choose your words carefully

Write down what you want remembered. Taking care about *how* you word it can increase the chances of people remembering it. Do not accept the first wording you can think of. Instead, try out variations until you find one that you are sure is right.

Make it catchy and concise.

We can all think of examples in advertising that have stuck, such as 'Just do it' by Nike.

In a seminar about image, executive speaking coach Jane D'Arcy summarised her ideas in an easy-to-recall phrase that she repeated: 'You attract whatever you radiate.'

Using a repeated word and the same letters to start words can work well, such as: 'It's all about the right people, the right products and the right processes.'

3 Choose *when* to repeat for most impact

Here are examples of good practice:

● *Say it at the start, middle and end*

This works because people more easily remember what's *first* and what is *last*. Saying it in the middle as well keeps it uppermost throughout.

● *Say it in a key section*

This example, from Winston Churchill's speech to the House of Commons in June 1940, shows how the repeated words, '*we shall,*' add great power to the ending. As you read the extract below, notice how the repetition of '*we shall*' conveys a real sense of purpose.

. . . 'we shall defend our Island, whatever the cost may be, we shall fight on the beaches, we shall fight on the landing grounds, we shall fight in the fields and in the streets, we shall fight in the hills; we shall never surrender' . . .

- *Say it sprinkled throughout*

  In every talk there are key moments that lend themselves to re-stating your message For instance, a great moment to repeat your message is immediately after you have given an example, or evidence that supports it. Repeating your message at this point makes complete sense logically and adds impact.

  'When you repeat and emphasize one idea, competing ideas are subordinated and sometimes are driven completely out of the audience's mind.'

  Jane D'Arcy, Executive Speech Coach

4 Say it in the same way

Use the same voice tone and emphasis to phrase it. The 'music' in your voice will help people remember it like a song. You may even find the audience start saying it back to you.

5 Make it visual to make it stick

Create a memorable link between what people hear and what they see. In one of his TED talks, Bill Gates had the phrase; 'Wanted – Energy Miracles' made into a slide with the words across a picture of the sky.

  Avoid over-repetition as it irritates – repeat it just enough to make it stick.

Your turn

For an existing or new talk:

1 Write down the most important take-away message.

2 Imagine what visual would enhance it.

3 Create a slide that combines the message with the picture.

Resource for further learning

'I have a dream speech', Martin Luther King Jr, YouTube (video clips or full speech 32 minutes).

Secret 39: Seven ways to make your voice easy to listen to

A voice that is easy to listen to makes a talk so much more enjoyable, but it may not be obvious how to achieve that. Surely we just speak the way we speak? There are a few simple techniques that can help you enhance the way you speak and increase your impact.

Why it matters

If your voice is not good, it can lead to a host of problems as a speaker. Being asked to repeat, or speak up can be embarrassing and reflect badly on you. A weak voice can adversely affect your credibility, while a good strong voice can boost it.

Fresh from his voice projection course, Colin made an instant impact on the team

What to do

In addition to *varying pace* and *pausing* (see Secret 40), the following will increase your impact:

1 Project your voice

Give it enough volume to suit the room size. Project your voice to the back of the room and you will soon gauge what is right. You need to be just loud enough that the audience are comfortably hearing you. They should neither be straining to hear nor feel you are raising your voice.

2 Speak clearly

It is easy to become lazy and run one word into the next. Do not rush your words. In a quickly spoken phrase, people can often miss parts of what you have said.

Lack of clarity often is caused by failing to sound the beginning and endings of words properly, for example, saying 'next Tuesday' as 'nexchoosdy.' If you now say 'next Tuesday' but really make sure you sound the 't' of 'next' and the 't' of Tuesday, you can feel your tongue on the roof of your mouth. You will create a slight gap between the words and they will be clearer. Pronounce beginnings and endings of words for greater clarity.

3 Let your voice rise and fall

We have all heard how boring a monotone voice can be. Vary the intonation by letting your voice rise and fall. When you speak with passion, the intonation will start to vary in a natural way.

4 Emphasise key words

Emphasis on a word makes your meaning clearer. Changing emphasis will change the meaning, such as 'It's *vital* that we support Derek on this very important project.' Compare that with: 'It's vital that we support Derek on this *very important project.'*

Go through presentation notes and highlight words and phrases to emphasise.

5 Avoid raising your voice at the end of sentences

This can diminish your authority. In fact, a high-pitched voice that also goes up at the end of a sentence can make the speaker sound nervous and even childish.

> **TIP**
>
> Replace 'ums' and 'filler words' with pauses.

6 Drop your voice at the end of a sentence to give more weight

It adds credibility. However, overdoing this can make you sound confrontational so reserve it for serious points.

7 Breathe deeply

Shallow breaths will not help project your voice and can lead to nervousness. Instead, breathe all the way down to your stomach, which is known as diaphragm breathing. Feel how your stomach moves out as you breathe in. This keeps airways clear and increases resonance. Resonance is the deep and strong quality of a reverberating voice.

Your turn

This exercise will enhance your speaking skills. You can do it alone or with someone to listen and give feedback.

1 Find a short article in a newspaper or a magazine.

2 Read it aloud for one minute and record your voice.

3 Listen back and review it. Identify what you do well and what you can do differently.

4 Read it again, putting into practice what you have learnt. Notice the difference.

5 Now read a different piece to develop your skills further.

Resource for further learning

'How to speak so that people want to listen' by Julian Treasure, TEDGlobal 2013 (10-minute video).

Includes expert tips on using your voice and is an outstanding example of how to deliver a talk. Observe especially his stance and how he uses gestures.

Secret 40: Create heightened attention to 'land' important points

Audiences will not remember everything you say, but, fortunately, the success of your talk is not dependent on them doing so. What is vital, however, is that they take away your key messages. Therefore, knowing how to 'land' important messages with impact is important.

Why it matters

- When you *say* it like it is important, your audience will *feel* its importance.

- A poorly delivered message dilutes its impact.

- When impact is weak, your message can be lost among supporting detail.

- When you 'land' the message well, you increase the chances of people taking action.

- When they understand the message, your talk is more likely to make the difference you desire.

When Donald's eyebrows went up, they knew he was about to say something important

What to do

Give the audience the sense that something important is coming up. Then say it in a way that conveys that importance.

The following will help you to do that.

1   Face the audience to make eye contact

If you were looking elsewhere, such as at the screen or your notes, make sure you turn to face the audience just before landing your point. Look at the audience and they will look at you. Then you have their full attention.

2   Stand upright

If, for any reason, you are not in an upright stance just before landing your key point, make sure you straighten up just before saying the phrase. Use the assertive, confident stance described in Secret 46.

TIP

Change your demeanour to one of seriousness just before making a serious point.

---

3   Build up to it

This starts to heighten attention as your phrasing creates anticipation before the big point itself, which is in italics in the example below.

'We lost market share last year.'

'And the competition this year is tougher than ever.'

'Therefore, if we want to stay in business we must always . . .'

'Put the customer first.'

4   Say it slowly and deliberately

Slow down the pace of the whole phrase to heighten its impact.

5   Stress the key word

Further slowing of one word will signify its importance.

- Say the key word more slowly.

- Say it with a lower pitch if you want to make it sound more serious.

Listen in your mind to how this phrase sounds when the word *always* is stressed:

- 'If we want to stay in business we must *always* put the customer first.'

It is the *contrast* between the way you say that word and the rest of the sentence that makes it stand out.

6 Pause before and after saying the key phrase

By pausing before and after your key message, you mark it out as important. Also pause before and after key words to create further impact.

Say the following message slowly with the pauses and notice how it sounds:

- 'If we want to be successful we must *always* (pause) put the customer first' (pause).

Pausing after the key point helps the message sink in.

7 Get the audience saying the message in their minds

Once you have said the key message a few times, the audience may anticipate it as you build up to it. Pause just before you say it and watch the audience say it in their minds, or they may say it out loud to you. This is known as 'call and response'.

Get into the habit of creating heightened attention for key messages.

Your turn

1 Next time you listen to the news, notice how key words and phrases are emphasised.

2 Practise emphasising key points in everyday conversation by being conscious of how you are using your voice.

3 Look at your notes for your next talk. Highlight words and phrases that must be especially emphasised. Practise saying them to get used to how you will deliver them.

Resource for further learning

'Bring your full voice to life' by Barbara McAfee, TEDxGustavusAdolphusCollege (19-minute video).

Secret 41: Try not to rush your words – or slow down too much

How fast should I speak? It is not pace itself that is the problem. It is keeping it at the *same* pace that you should avoid because it can sound monotonous. Instead, *vary your pace.*

Why it matters

The rate at which you speak matters because:

1 If you are speaking *too slowly*:

- the audience may become impatient and want you to 'get a move on';
- research shows you can come across as less intelligent;
- you can come across as boring.

2 If you are speaking *too quickly*:

- you can be perceived as nervous;
- it can sound as if you are hurrying;
- the audience do not get a chance to absorb your words.

What to do

Research often divides rate of speech into:

- *Slow:* 110 words or per minute or less;

Since he started using a racing commentator microphone, Jeff could fit a one-hour briefing into 10 minutes

- *Conversational:* 120–150 words per minute;
- *Fast:* 160 plus words per minute with upper limit around 180.

Newsreaders speak at around 150 words per minute and, on average, the same rate of speech applies to audio books. This pace enables listeners to digest what is being said.

However, it is not all about rate of speaking. Andrew Dlugan, speaking coach and founder of public speaking website 'Six Minutes', analysed nine popular TED talks. He found the average rate to be 163 words per minute, with the lowest at 133 and highest at 188.

Research published in the *Journal of Personality and Social Psychology* found that those who spoke more quickly generally were perceived as more credible. Furthermore, 'the fast speaker was seen as more knowledgeable and trustworthy'. ('Speed of Speech and Persuasion' (1976) by Miller, Maruyama, Beaber and Valone University of California in *Journal of Personality and Social Pyschology,* Vol. 34, No. 4).

However, such research should not be your cue to speed up too much, but rather to caution you against going *too* slowly.

> *Nothing seems to undermine the credibility more than a speaker with long 'thought-pauses', except, perhaps, one whose pauses are filled with 'Errrr'.*

Simon Raybould, author of Presentation Genius

John F. Kennedy was a fast speaker. However, in his inaugural address, he slowed his pace to around 97 words per minute. Martin Luther King Jr.'s 'I have a dream' speech was around 98 words per minute. His speech was rated as the number one speech of the twentieth century in an academic poll.

> *Even the slowest great speakers have quick phrases and the fast ones have slow phrases. And they all have pauses.*

To speak in an engaging way:

1 **You probably need to speak more slowly than you think**
   I say this because most people I coach need to speak more slowly than they realise. This applies especially if you are a natural 'speed talker'. To find out if you really do need to slow down, do the exercise in 'Your turn' below.

2 **Aim for a conversational pace**

TIP

If in doubt, slow down.

Chris Anderson, Head of TED, makes the point that most of us are not delivering a rousing speech to an audience of several hundred thousand. Therefore, to slow down to Martin Luther King pace is inappropriate for most situations.

> *Overall you should plan to speak at your natural conversational pace.*

Chris Anderson, Head of TED

3 Vary the pace

Using slow, medium and fast speeds keeps it interesting. Slow down for serious points or tricky explanations, then speed up to inject excitement, urgency and passion or perhaps tell a humorous anecdote.

4 Pause

Pausing breaks up content into bite-sized chunks that are easier to grasp. A pause can create drama and give an audience a chance to reflect on what has just been said. Pauses help you to 'land' key points and you can learn more about that in Secret 40.

5 Do not force a big change of pace – make slight adjustments

Forcing a big change of your overall pace can make you sound unnatural. Instead, try either increasing or decreasing by a little.

6 Slow down for increased power and resonance

Slow down to convey key messages with impact. You create power and resonance (a deep reverberating sound) by speaking more slowly. When speaking too quickly you lose that rich quality. Slowing down allows you to put so much more meaning into your words.

7 If you sense you are too fast, take a deep breath

Some people speak so fast they hardly have time to catch their breath and the audience feel the sense of hurrying too. An easy way to slow down is to breathe deeply.

Your turn

1 Record your voice and play it back to hear how fast you speak.

2 Next time you give a talk, ask for feedback about your rate of speaking.

3 Decide if you need to make any adjustments.

Resource for further learning

To see the contrast between a slower and a faster rate of speech, take a look at the following examples:

- *Slower:* John F. Kennedy's 'We choose to go to the moon speech', 1963, YouTube, (video clips from 2 minutes). This is an example of a slower speech at around 99 words per minute.

- *Faster:* 'Inspiring a life of immersion' by Jacqueline Novogratz, TEDWomen 2010 (17-minute video). This is an example of a faster speech at 188 words per minute.

Secret 42: The art of framing and reframing

Nothing is either good or bad but thinking makes it so.

Shakespeare's *Hamlet*

Framing is the act of presenting something so that people see it from a particular viewpoint. For example, customer complaints may be framed as 'helpful' because they offer a chance to learn and improve.

Reframing is when we *change* our perspective or that of others. For example, 'It's too bad I didn't get the job.' In reply, a friend might reframe this by saying: 'It obviously wasn't the right one for you.' This changes the way of thinking about what happened and may cause the person to feel more positive.

Use framing and reframing when you want to influence the way the audience looks at something.

Why it matters

Framing and reframing can help you to:

- set expectations;

- encourage the audience to see your ideas in a certain way;

- create the frame of mind you want, such as curiosity, open mindedness or concern;

- lessen the chances of resistance to your ideas;

- shift the focus from negative to positive.

Colin's attempt to put a positive spin on results had some way to go to convince the team

What to do

We will look at each in turn:

1 Framing

Frames can be set at the start and part way through a talk.

Here are example phrases for framing and what they achieve:

- *'This talk is an overview.'*

  Lets people know not to expect detail.

- *'I don't profess to have all the answers.'*

  Means they should not be surprised if there is a question you cannot answer.

- *'You will know best which of the techniques will help you the most in your own work.'*

  Frames your session as not *telling* them what to do but giving *choice*.

See Secret 43 to see how framing can be applied to minimise objections.

The frames you set will help you to smooth the way for a successful presentation.

2 Reframing

Use a reframe to shift perspective when:

● an audience member makes a comment that may not be helpful to your desired outcome, the needs of the audience or even their own needs;

● people are 'stuck' or feel there is not much they can do about something;

● someone asks a question with a negative emphasis and you want to respond in a positive way.

Here are examples of what people might say and how you could respond with a reframe:

Comment: 'It is so difficult to solve this problem.'

Reframe: 'What would success look like?'

This changes perspective from a 'problem frame' to an 'outcome frame.'

Comment: 'There's nothing we can do about this.'

Reframe: ''Who could help?'

This changes the view from impossibility to one of possibility.

Comment: 'There is no answer to this.'

Reframe: 'If you had a magic wand, what would help?'

This shifts the view to an imaginative perspective.

Comment: 'We are stuck.'

Reframe: ''What would be the first step forward?'

This changes focus from helplessness to being able to at least make a start.

Comment: 'We can never get that done in three weeks.'

Reframe: 'Just imagine if we had done. How did we do it?'

This moves to an 'as-if' frame, so let's think 'as-if' we already did it.

Be ready to use reframes when it would be helpful to change the focus.

Your turn

1   Practise reframing in everyday conversation; when you hear someone placing a meaning on an experience, ask a question that helps them focus on the positives.

2   Listen out for reframes in meetings and conversations.

3   Write down phrases you could use in your introduction that will frame how you want people to view your talk.

Resource for further learning

NLP Workbook: A Practical Guide to Achieving the Results you Want (2001) by Joseph O'Connor.

See Chapter 15 'Framing' for guidance on many different ways of framing.

Secret 43: How to minimise potential objections

No matter how well you plan your presentation it is natural that people may raise objections. Some people are extremely good at thinking of reasons why your idea may not work. We need to be able to handle objections, but it is so much better if we can prevent most of them occurring in the first place.

Why it matters

With a little forethought, you can prevent many objections.

This matters because:

- not thinking of objections causes unnecessary problems;
- too many objections can make you look like you have not thought things through;
- people may also see you as unprofessional or lacking knowledge about your subject;
- handling difficult objections without prior thought can be more challenging;
- your credibility can quickly decrease when you are struggling to respond;
- anticipating concerns increases the audience's confidence in you.

By the fifth objection, Mary realised she should have thought more in advance

Failing to anticipate audience objections can lead to an uncomfortable time on the day.

What to do

1 Write down all the possible objections you can think of

- Imagine you are an audience member. Go through your talk and identify points that people might query or challenge you on.

- Ask a colleague to think of the worst possible questions that might come up.

2 Plan how you will cover these in your talk

- Identify where to address each potential objection in your talk.

- Decide what will convince your audience. It could be evidence, examples or facts.

- Write down what you need to say or show the audience to deal with the issue.

3 Flag up that everything might not be perfect

Here are some framing tips to minimise objections, or at least encourage people to challenge in a helpful way. See Secret 42 for more on framing.

Phrasing examples:

- 'I'd ask you to consider an idea. It's not fully formed, but I'd be interested to hear what you think.'

- 'Here's a first shot at a solution that Jim and I came up with. We're not totally convinced about it, so I'd appreciate your thoughts.'

- 'I'm going to show you the latest project plan. We've thought it through as much as we can, but there could be a few glitches. If you spot any, please say.'

4 Frame points that people might object to – just before you present them

If you sense there may be objections to what you are about to say, you can frame it to make objections less likely, as in these examples.

● When your suggestion is the opposite of what might seem sensible:

The framing phrase: 'The following suggestion might seem counter-intuitive, but I'd like you to keep an open mind.'

The positive effect: People are more likely to keep an open mind.

● When you think people might be sceptical of what you are about to say:

The framing phrase: 'Here's an idea that I was sceptical about when I first heard it. It might seem a bit strange to you, too.'

The positive effect: They are less likely to challenge because you were also sceptical, Furthermore, the phrase: 'when I first heard it,' suggests that the idea may seem strange only initially.

● When you think people might find your statistic implausible.

The framing phrase: 'Here's an amazing statistic. When I first heard it, I thought "This can't be true".'

The positive effect: Most people will be less likely to say they do not believe it because you also said that you doubted it.

Your turn

1 Look at your notes for a talk and identify one point that people might challenge.

2 Write down what you could say in advance to make a challenge less likely or at least influence people to be constructive in the way they challenge.

3 In everyday conversation or meetings, when you are about to suggest an idea people may not agree with, say something in advance to encourage them to be more open.

Resource for further learning

Personal Impact: What it Takes to Make a Difference (2009) by Amanda Vickers, Steve Bavister and Jackie Smith.

Chapter 6 'Influence with impact' has tips on persuasion that can be applied to minimising objections.

Secret 44: Choose your words carefully when explaining change

Change can be stressful. Explaining it without making people feel worse can be difficult. The words you use are an important factor in getting people on board; research shows that a little attention to our choice of words makes a big difference.

Karen wondered why the team weren't up for the change, apart from Jeff, who likes to do something different every day

Why it matters

The research of Rodger Bailey, creator of the Language and Behaviour (LAB) Profile, gives important insights into how to speak about change, if we want to influence people to accept it. The LAB Profile is a tool that helps us understand and influence behaviour.

His work is reported by Shelle Rose Charvet in her book *Words That Change Minds* and the key findings in relation to change are:

- Only around 20 per cent of people like *frequent change*. Every year or so, they like a big change in their work, such as the chance to do something different.

- Approximately 65 per cent of people like things to remain *largely the same*, except for every year or two when they will accept moderate change, such as enhancements to their role.

- The remaining 15 per cent are split between liking either *extreme* sameness or various *combinations* of sameness and difference.

   Therefore, when explaining change, use words that appeal to the bigger percentages.

What to do

Just like in golf – play the 'percentage shot' as a rule.

The 'percentage shot' is the safe shot. When a golf ball is in the rough, do not risk trying to bend a shot around a tree. Just chip the ball safely back onto the fairway.

When this is applied to explaining change, it means explaining your point in a way that appeals to the 65 per cent. You can do so in the knowledge that a further 20 per cent who would be happy with even greater change will take it in their stride. You will be appealing to around 85 per cent of your audience.

1   Avoid words and phrases that emphasise the differences

Examples include: change; changing; new; you will be working totally differently; or it will revolutionise your job.

2   Explain what is staying the same

Use phrases like: it's just like; the process is basically the same; it's very similar to what we do now; or it's exactly like.

3 Explain differences with words that signify evolving change

Use words like: improving, refining, upgrading, better, quicker, growing, enhancing and developing.

TIP

Make a list of suitable words and phrases in advance of speaking.

An example of how to explain change is given by author Shelle Rose Charvet. Many years ago, typewriters were replaced by word processors. Imagine having to explain that change to people who had used typewriters for many years and who were apprehensive about using word processors.

If you described the change by *emphasising differences and newness,* this would appeal only to the 20 per cent who really like change. It would worry the majority if you said:

- 'It's all new.'
- 'It is a big change.'
- 'There are lots of different things to learn.'
- 'It's a revolution in the way you will work.'
- 'Your job will never be the same.'

Instead, if you used words that *highlight similarities and enhancements*: this would appeal to the 65 per cent who prefer moderate change. Furthermore, the 20 per cent who are happy with big changes will be fine because this small degree of change will be no big deal to them.

The following phrases would encourage the majority to feel more comfortable about moving from typewriter to a word processor:

- 'The computer screen is like a piece of paper.'
- 'The keys are mostly all the same.'
- 'The word processor is like a typewriter.'

- 'It's easier to correct mistakes.'
- 'New documents are quicker to create because you can base them on your old ones without retyping it all again.'

Take time to choose your words carefully when explaining change.

Your turn

1   Think of a change you may have to explain to a group.
2   Use some of the following words to create phrases for your presentation: improving, refining, upgrading, better, quicker, growing, enhancing and developing.
3   Decide where in the beginning, middle and end you will use these phrases.

Resource for further learning

Words That Change Minds: Mastering the Language of Influence (1995) by Shelle Rose Charvet.

Secret 45: Yes, Richard, I remember your name

Have you had the experience of someone using your name when you did not expect it? It can make you feel special, impressed and valued, but many of us do not think we can remember names.

Why it matters

The numerous benefits of remembering names include:

- It feels personal.
- People feel important.
- You build rapport.
- It helps your credibility.

Bob thought he'd probably overdone it on the size of the name badges

What to do

What stops us remembering names? When we say we cannot remember a name, usually we never really learnt it in the first place.

Have you ever been introduced to someone and then, seconds later, cannot recall their name? You probably did not take in the name properly originally. Just like any filing system, if want to get information *out,* you first have to put information *in.*

1   Do something *actively* with the name to make it easier to recall

Actively taking the name in involves using different senses: *seeing, hearing, saying* and *doing,* all of which help our memory.

Follow these steps when meeting someone new. The steps help to *slow down* the introduction process and make it easier to learn their name.

- **Look directly to make eye contact** with the person and say: 'Hello, I'm . . . (your name) and you are . . . ?'

  (*saying* and *seeing*)

- **Shake hands**

  (*doing*)

- **Keep looking** at them as you shake hands – because seeing their face as they say their name helps you remember.

  (*seeing*)

- **Listen** as they say their name: 'I'm Mary.'

  Keep looking at them as they say their name.

  (*seeing* and *hearing*)

- **Repeat** their name: 'Great to meet you, Mary.'

  (*saying*)

- **Use the name again soon after** to introduce them to others: 'Ah, Gerry, do you know Mary?'

  (*repeating again*)

TIP

Remind yourself ahead of time that you intend to remember names.

---

2   **Five ways to reinforce your memory of someone's name**

- **Look at their name badge, if they have one**

  Notice its spelling or anything odd that will help your memory. There might be a surname that helps as well.

- **Ask them how to spell their name**

  An understandable reason could be:

  - there is no name badge;

- the name is unusual;

- there are two ways of spelling it.

You can justify the question by saying that the spelling helps you remember. You might ask:

- 'Is that Catherine with a C or a K?'

- 'I've never heard that name before . . . how do you spell it?'

- **Make an imaginative association**

  Notice anything special about the name itself or the person's appearance.

  - Their name is the same as a friend: imagine your friend alongside.

  - Their name is the same as a famous golfer: imagine them with golf clubs.

  - Their name is also the name of a place.

  - They resemble someone famous.

- **Write down their name**

  - The act of writing it down will reinforce memory.

  - If numbers are low enough to do so, write everyone's name on paper in the position they are seated in the room.

- **Keep looking back at people to see if you can put names to faces**

  Look across the room and check that you can name those you have already met.

3 **What if I forget a name?**

- Ask someone else who you think might know.

4 **What if it is a big audience?**

You almost certainly will not meet the audience individually and would not be expected to know names anyway. However, still try to use names when you can.

● **Use people's names when they ask questions**
   Ask them their name, then say it in your reply.

Just have a go – you will soon be able to recall 20 or more names easily as people arrive at your talk.

Your turn

1   Next time you are at a social gathering with people you do not know, practise the six steps to help you learn their names.

2   When you are being served in a shop by someone with a name badge, use their name.

3   When you are in a restaurant, ask the waiter or waitress their name and then use it.

Resource for further learning

How to Develop a Brilliant Memory Week by Week: 50 Proven Ways to Enhance Your Memory Skills (2014) by Dominic O' Brien.

Includes: 'How to Remember Names and Faces' and much more.

7

What to do and how to do it

Secret 46: How to stand to enhance your impact

People naturally want to stand in a way that feels comfortable. Some like to stand casually with their weight on one leg, some bolt upright, while others prefer to wander about. What's the problem? you might ask. Surely it is just a case of personal preference?

The problem is that we need to be concerned primarily with how our stance appears to the audience. Our own preferences should not override that.

Why it matters

Here are the key reasons:

- Everything you do conveys a message – including your stance.

- People form an impression of you very quickly – stance is a big part of that.

- Your posture can either dilute a message or give it more gravitas.

- Stance can diminish or increase your credibility and authority.

- When you change posture you change how you feel, which affects how you act.

- If you stand confidently, it boosts your confidence.

Brian's updates were entertaining, but the team did wonder about his balletic postures

How you stand and move has a major impact on how you come across to the audience

What to do

1 Stand centre-stage whenever possible

The most influential place is the centre of the stage. The red circle for TED speakers is typically in the centre.

This works best because:

- the centre at the front is the most powerful and influential place in the room;
- if you relegate yourself to one side, your message does not have the full impact;
- your points come across as more important when spoken from the centre.

2 Use the assertive stance most, or all, of the time

By using the assertive stance you come across as:

- credible;
- professional;
- competent;
- confident;
- assertive.

Here is how:

Feet – give a solid base

- Place your feet hip-width apart.
- Have your toes pointing slightly outwards.

Legs

- Stand upright – legs straight – avoid leaning.
- Avoid locking your knees because this will soon feel uncomfortable. Just loosen the knees slightly, yet maintain an upright posture.
- Avoid shifting your weight from one side to the other or swaying.

Hips

- Keep hips square and in horizontal alignment, so your body is not dropping to one side.

Hands

- Most of the time, you will be using your hands for gesturing.
- However, when you are not, for example, while waiting for the audience to settle, just drop your hands by your side. It might feel slightly strange at first, but it looks fine.

Head

- Hold your head up confidently.

> *Having your head balanced evenly on your shoulders, with your eyes looking forward and everything upright, conveys confidence.*
>
> Amanda Vickers, Steve Bavister and Jackie Smith, authors of
> *Personal Impact*

Generally, I suggest staying in this assertive stance for your entire presentation, including questions.

However, the casual stance described below is also helpful to have as an option for the specific reasons given.

3   Use a casual stance at times, but *only* if and when appropriate

You might stand casually when you want to appear more:

● approachable;

● informal;

● relaxed;

● friendly;

● amiable.

Here is how:

● weight more on one leg;

● one knee bent and the other leg straight;

● head at an angle when listening to questions;

● one hand may be on the chin when listening;

● or hands may be at your sides.

This is useful when:

● chatting to the group in a more relaxed manner;

● listening to a question. However, remaining in the assertive stance for questions is often still the best choice because it maintains your authority.

TIP

Use the casual stance to listen, then straighten up into the confident stance to answer it. This will give your answer more authority.

---

4 Do not walk about, unless for a specific purpose

Some speakers walk about and make it work. However, wandering for no particular reason usually will make it harder for the audience to listen and make you look less credible.

Imagine you are in the TED talk red circle and stay there.

5 What if the screen is in the centre and I cannot stand there?

Position yourself slightly to one side while showing visuals, but move to the centre at other times.

6 What about sitting down?

I recommend standing whenever possible because it gives you more authority. However, you might sometimes *choose* to be seated. For example, when speaking to just several people it can seem friendlier to sit down. There might be times when you *have to stay seated*. In this case, if at all possible, ensure that you can easily make eye contact with all in the room. This will help you to be more influential than if you have to keep swivelling. You could give a reason why it would help if you sat at the front while you speak. You may even be able to request that some people move their seat or change seats.

The speaking skills described for standing can easily be adapted for sitting. For example, sit upright to convey authority, use gestures to help explain your ideas, make eye contact, and so on.

Your turn

1 Practise standing in the assertive stance on other occasions, such as in conversations.

2 Then adjust to the casual stance.

3 Feel the difference.

Resource for further learning

Personal Impact: What it Takes to Make a Difference (2009) by Amanda Vickers, Steve Bavister and Jackie Smith.

Chapter 7 'Body Talk' to learn more about how body language makes a difference.

Secret 47: How to make eye contact and connect with everyone

The value of making good eye contact is immense, yet for many speakers, it is a real problem. Some speakers try to avoid direct eye contact, while others are not sure where to look. The fact is that if you do not make eye contact, you are missing a big trick. In this Secret, we learn exactly how to do it, whatever the size of audience.

Why it matters

● **It builds rapport**

As people arrive, you may have the chance to say hello and shake hands. After that, there is no direct contact, but eye contact is a way to continue that connection.

● **You get immediate feedback**

If you look at the audience, you will get instant feedback on how your talk is going. Changes in facial expressions of the audience tell you how people are reacting.

● **People feel like you are speaking just to them**

With good eye contact, people feel a personal connection.

● **It keeps your attention 'out there'**

Eye contact keeps your focus on the audience instead of being 'in your head' and over-thinking, which can cause anxiousness. When our attention is 'out there', it helps us stay in the moment, so we perform better.

Avoiding eye contact is not the answer.

What to do

1 **Do not:**

● sweep from side to side like the beam of a lighthouse;

● flit about with glances;

● stare or hold your gaze too long on one person.

Unsure of where to look, Barbara found that her gaze had fixated on the exit sign

2   Make direct eye contact with each person

If the size of the audience permits, make direct eye contact with everyone.

3   Move eye contact from person to person randomly

Rather than using an ordered sequence, such as left to right across a row of people, make eye contact in a random fashion and this will look more natural.

4   Make eye contact with specific people when it is relevant to do so

Do this when what you are saying relates to an audience member. For example, 'As Derek here would no doubt tell you.'

5   Hold eye contact for as long as it feels instinctively right

This is not an exact science. Just as in conversation, move your gaze to another person when it feels right.

6   What if the audience is too large to make eye contact with everyone?

Graham Davies, author of *The Presentation Coach*, advises: 'You should *not* be aiming for eye contact. You should be aiming for the *illusion* of eye contact.'

Mentally divide the audience into groups such as left, middle and right. Look at someone in one of the groups and the whole group will feel as if you are looking at them. Move around groups randomly to cover the entire audience.

You will usually still need to look at people individually if they are at the front because often they are too close to be viewed in a group.

TIP

Keep up a connection with people at the back by making eye contact.

---

7 What do I do when someone is asking a question?

Give your undivided attention to that person to demonstrate that you are listening and value their question.

8 What about eye contact when I am answering the question?

If it is a very short answer, just look at the person who asked the question. For a longer answer, include the rest of the audience as well. See Secret 58 on managing questions for more guidance on eye contact for questions.

Practise making eye contact in groups and it will become natural.

Your turn

1 Awareness exercise

Notice how well people use eye contact. When someone speaks, do they connect with eye contact? When people listen, do they maintain eye contact with the person talking?

2 Informal practice

It is helpful to practise during social settings. See how well you can use eye contact when you are speaking and listening.

3   Noticing what other speakers do

Next time you have a chance, notice how well the speaker does at keeping everyone engaged with eye contact.

Resource for further learning

The Presentation Coach: Bare Knuckle Brilliance For Every Presenter (2010) by Graham Davies.

Chapter 9 'Control Yourself' has advice on eye contact and many other aspects of speaking.

Secret 48: Use descriptive gestures to show what you mean

What do I do with my hands? Use your hands in a natural way and people will understand you more easily. Gesturing is also proven to help us to be more articulate.

Why it matters

Reasons for using gestures:

- Descriptive gestures 'paint' pictures so the audience literally 'see' what you mean.

- It is less mental effort for people to understand you compared with when you do not use gestures.

- Gestures add conviction and help you bring ideas alive with emotion.

- Research by Robert Krauss at Columbia University found that gesturing helps us marshal our thoughts, find our words and be more fluent. Hold your arms still and by your side while trying to explain something. Most people find it difficult and say they feel that they want to move their hands.

By gesturing you not only unfreeze your body – you unfreeze your mind.

Olivia Mitchell, speaking coach

Donald's gestures helped paint a mental picture, but they did not always convince his audience

What to do

1 Use your hands as you would naturally

Just let your hands move as you would in normal conversation. By rehearsing, you will find yourself repeating the gestures that work well.

2 Paint pictures with gestures

Let your gestures paint pictures. You can describe size, movement, shape and much more. Be literal, for example, a winding river needs a winding gesture to give a visual sense and a feel for it.

3 Describe abstract concepts with gestures too

Just as we use gestures to paint pictures of concrete things, we can do the same with abstract concepts, so an upward gesture can show an upward trend.

4 Allow 'daylight' between arms and body

Do not keep your upper arms 'stuck' to your body; it looks odd and restricts the width of gestures

Instead, move your arms away from you so there is 'daylight' between your arms and body; it looks much better

5 Make your gestures the right size

Describing a house with small gestures makes it look like a doll's house. Instead, make your gestures reflect the size of what you are describing. A big mountain requires a big gesture and a tiny insect needs a small gesture.

6 Use the full 'canvas'

If you do not open up your gestures, it is like an artist with a huge canvas who paints only in the middle of it. Instead, open your arms wide to find the full width of your canvas. This is the range of your gestures. It might feel big, but to the audience it looks fine.

7 Be clear and deliberate

Do not make really fast gestures or flit about. When you do this, it is like a television picture shimmering and people cannot follow so well. The exception is when you are purposely describing something that really is very fast or erratic.

8 Hold a gesture still to maximise the effect

To indicate something solid like a wall, you need to hold your gesture still. You may have seen a mime artist pretending to be inside a box. They 'push' their hands against the sides of the imaginary box. This is a good example of holding a gesture.

9 Keep your gestures 'above the counter'

When shopkeepers are behind the counter, you see their hands only when they lift them above it. Imagine you are a shopkeeper and make all your gestures 'above the counter'. The exception is when you are making a low gesture for a specific reason.

10 When gesturing with one arm keep the other by your side

You want people to focus only on the gesturing arm so keep the other arm still at your side.

Your turn

1 Practise gestures in social conversation.

2 Next time someone asks you to explain something, practise gestures.

3 When in a group, notice gestures.

4 Watch how speakers and TV presenters use gestures.

Resource for further learning

The Definitive Book of Body Language: How to Read Others' Attitudes by Their Gestures (2017) by Allan and Barbara Pease.

Chapter 11 'The 13 most common gestures you'll see daily'.

Secret 49: How gestures can demonstrate timelines

When people look at a graph with a timeline on the horizontal axis, the time is shown to flow from left to right. In the same way, you should

Jane had a unique way to help her remember which direction to make her timeline gestures

gesture towards the audience's left to indicate the *past* and to their right to indicate the *future*. When you make these gestures in the correct direction it makes a difference because it intuitively makes sense to the audience.

Why it matters

Using the appropriate gestures for timelines and continuums will:

- allow you to mark out a timeline visually;
- just *look* and *feel* right to the audience;
- help them grasp time-related ideas much more easily;
- enable you to refer again to a point in time with a gesture in the same place. This is known as 'anchoring' because you are 'fixing' an idea to that space. When you gesture to it again, people instantly bring that idea to mind.

No one will *consciously* notice what you are doing, but it impacts on they experience your talk. It is an example of how everything counts, so why do it wrong if we can do it right?

What to do

Imagine time represented as a line across the stage. From the audience's viewpoint we have:

Past   Present   Future

So we have a timeline that people instinctively understand. If you asked where the *past* was, most people in the audience would point to the left.

We can match our gestures to the timeline to emphasise points. With a gesture we can refer to the past, present, future.

N.B. Our natural tendency is to make gestures from *our* viewpoint instead of that of the audience. When *facing* an audience remember to *switch your natural direction* for the gestures.

Thus when facing the audience from the stage, the correct way to make gestures is:

Gesture to the *audience's left* **to indicate** *the past*

Gesture *in the centre* **to indicate the** *present*

Gesture to the *audience's right* to indicate *the future*

TIP

Practise: because you are reversing what you would normally do.

Use this technique to explain numerous time-related ideas.

Time-related examples

Explaining a project timeline:

Start   Where we are now   What happens next

Explaining a vision:

Where we were   Where we are now   The future vision

Explaining a project timeline:

Since February we've been doing. . .	Today we are here. . .	As a result of today we will . . .

Calibrated continuum examples

You can mentally put numbers on your timelines. Then you can use gestures to explain that continuum.

Zero	50	100

Contrast examples

You can make use of the timeline when you are talking about opposing ideas.

> *Gestures like holding out one hand to one side of your body and then later the other hand on the other side help the audience to separate ideas and concepts.*
>
> Gavin Meikle, author of *The Presenter's Edge*

Typically, it is helpful to represent the ideas in the past and future spaces as indicated below.

Past	*Future*
Negatives	Positives
Bad	Good
Problems	Solutions
Wrong	Right
Cons	Pros

> *Once you get into the habit of using gestures in this way, it will become natural.*

Your turn

Develop your skill:

● Next time you are in conversation with someone sitting opposite you, practise using time gestures in this way. It will help you to practise remembering to switch your natural direction of gesturing to suit the listener.

Resource for further learning

The Presenter's Edge: How to Unlock Your Inner Speaker (2016) by Gavin Meikle.

Chapter 7 'The Visual Channel' gives guidance on different kinds of gestures and other aspects of body language.

Secret 50: Use gestures to emphasise points and connect with the audience

A gesture can quickly change the feeling in the room, so with the right gestures, you can change the mood to match your message. Gestures also create powerful connections between you and the group or individuals within it.

Why it matters

Gestures can help us to:

- connect with people and build the relationship;
- convey emotions;
- quickly change the mood from light to serious or vice versa;
- enable us to reinforce important messages;
- lessen resistance and increase rapport;
- look professional in the way we interact;
- change our own state.

After 30 minutes and no sign of his hands, the team thought Mike might be hiding something from them

What to do

1 Connect with one person or a section of the audience

Gesture towards the person, or section of audience, and hold it for a few seconds as shown in the top picture on the next page.

This is useful at question time, or any other time you want to invite a comment. It is also useful whenever you want to make a comment to an individual or a particular section of the audience.

2 Connect to the whole audience

Open your arms out to the side as shown in the lower picture on the next page.

This gesture creates a sense of 'we' rather than 'you' and 'them'. Therefore, it is appropriate for emphasising your connection with the audience. It is also useful when saying 'welcome' or 'thank you'.

Use greeting gestures to develop and increase rapport.

3 Palms down to increase credibility

Use downward movement with both hands as you emphasise your points.

This is useful to change the mood to one of seriousness and emphasise a point. It is helpful when saying that something *must* happen or stating a fact that *cannot* be argued with.

- 'It's really important that we all do this.'

- 'It will take two weeks and it can't be done in less.'

- 'This is how it has to be done.'

When you use palms-down gestures, together with a serious voice, you decrease the chances of being challenged. Do not over-use it, but keep it for serious messages.

4 Palms up to increase approachability

Just explain things naturally and your palms will be upwards a lot of the time anyway. Your voice usually will follow your gestures and sound more upbeat than with palms down.

Listen to the upbeat voice in your head as you read the phrases below, which work well if you hold your arms with palms up.

- 'So that's all there is to it.'

- 'Just give it a try and see for yourself.'
- 'Why not? It's worth exploring, isn't it?'

> **TIP**
>
> Change your physiology to change your state. Try it now: palms up/palms down – feel the difference!

5 Keep hands visible

Do not put your hands behind your back or in your pockets. Behind the back can signal nervousness or that you are hiding something. Hands in pockets may be interpreted as too casual.

6 Keep body space clear when not gesturing

Having your hands across the front of your body when you are not gesturing does not generally look good. Avoid clasped hands or 'fiddling' which can make you look nervous.

Avoid keeping hands in front like this when not gesturing

Arms at sides and your body space clear looks much better

As advised in Secret 46, it looks much more professional to just drop your arms by your side.

7   What to be careful about

- *Do not point* at people or anything else. Merely pointing the finger and having the hand in that gun shape is enough to send negative energy.

- *Worse still is to wag your finger!* Always gesture toward anything or anyone with that open-handed gesture described above.

Your turn

1   Practise using gestures to connect with people in social situations.

2   Next time you make a serious point in conversation, emphasise it with a 'palms down' gesture.

3   Then turn your palms back upwards as you continue speaking.

Resource for further learning

The Leader's Guide to Presenting: How to Use Soft Skills to Get Hard Results (2017) by Tom Bird and Jeremy Cassell.

Chapter 13 'Developing your credibility as a presenter' includes research and guidance on body language.

Secret 51: Be credible, yet know when to be approachable

When you can successfully flex between being credible and approachable you will be more persuasive and increase your chances of getting the outcome you want.

Why it matters

Some people come across as highly credible and convey an air of authority. Others are very approachable and appear much more amiable.

Author and expert in non-verbal communication, Michael Grinder, uses the terms 'credible cats' and 'approachable dogs' to highlight the difference between the two. We can appeal to dogs by being nice to them. Cats, however, are more independent. A person who is a 'credible' cat just wants us to get to the point. However, an 'approachable dog' will appreciate a friendly style.

Being able to use both credible and approachable styles enables you to:

- match your style to your message;

- adjust your style to the audience;

- build rapport more quickly;

- give your points appropriate impact;

- respond to what is happening in the moment;

- quickly change the rhythm and mood of a talk;

- increase the chance of achieving your outcome.

Karen was so flexible in her presentation style that she could appeal equally well to the credible cats and the approachable dogs

What to do

Be prepared to use both credible and approachable styles.

Credibility is characterised by: an upright stance, little body movement, serious voice, often dropping at the end of sentences, serious facial expression, more palm-down gestures and a to-the-point delivery.

Approachability typically features: more body movement, melodic, varied and friendly voice tone and pitch, more palms-up and expansive gestures, more smiles and more detail in what you say.

To be a successful speaker in your field, you *must* come across as credible. This is why I advise *keeping in an upright stance throughout a talk.*

> *Use credibility as your base and add approachability as required.*

However, the ability also to be approachable adds so much and is part of the repertoire of many great speakers.

Use a more *credible style* when:

1 Opening your talk

It is safer to start by being credible to establish that you are an authority and are trustworthy.

2 You anticipate resistance

Trying to be too nice can cause people not to take you seriously.

3 You know the audience will favour a credible style

I have presented to military personnel and airline flight crew and both groups appreciate being spoken to in a predominantly credible style.

4 Explaining facts, key messages, research, data

To be convincing, your style must match the solid points you are making.

5 Making a very serious point

A key point about safety requires you to look and sound highly credible.

Use a more *approachable style* when:

1 You know the audience are highly approachable

I have presented to airline cabin crew who tend to be highly outgoing, talkative and sociable. An emphasis on the approachable style works well with them.

2 Telling stories and anecdotes

An approachable style enables you to bring stories to life using a varied voice and body language.

3 Involved in witty 'off-the-cuff' interactions

Moving away from credible style is in keeping with being playful, but be careful not to be over-familiar.

4 You want to lighten the mood

Changing your own state helps the audience to change theirs.

5 Seeking ideas from the audience

A more friendly and curious manner will often help when asking and listening.

TIP

If in doubt, be more credible – you can always ease off and be more approachable.

Your turn

Practise being flexible in your style:

1 Are you naturally more credible or more approachable? Write down what you think.

2 Explain the characteristics of both styles to a friend. Then ask them which they think is most like you.

3 Next time you are in conversation, notice the style of the other person and adapt your style a little to be more similar to theirs.

Resource for further learning

Charisma: The Art of Relationships – Understanding the 'cats' and 'dogs' in our lives – an analogy (2010) by Michael Grinder.

Secret 52: Make them eager to see the next slide

It is common practice to *show the slide first* and then explain it once it is up on the screen. Instead, in most cases, say something about it first.

Introduce the slide before revealing it.

Why it matters

Showing the slide first often leads to audience attention wandering because people instantly try to make sense of it. Even doing this for a few seconds can take their minds away from the important message.

As a rule, *introduce the slide before you show it* because it:

● alerts them to *focus their attention instantly* on the important part;

● gives the *context* of the slide so people understand it better;

● increases *curiosity,* which research has shown to boost learning;

● *motivates* people to want to see it;

● *creates links* between slides, which makes them easier to follow.

What to do

1   Introduce the slide

This will alert people to what is coming up. Most people like to *get the big picture first* and then the detail.

Example phrasing:

● **Create a strong link between the last slide and this one**

● 'So that was the old system. Now let's look at the new one.'

Cathy always found ways to make the team keen to see her next slide

- 'Having seen the overall project plan, we'll now look at each of the four stages.'

- 'Moving on to look at the implementation phase. . . '

● **Tell them what you are about to show**

- 'The next slide will show a map of the new site.'

- 'Now let's look at the sales in the last year.'

- 'Here are the results of our customer survey.'

● **Increase motivation to look at the next slide**

- 'You might be surprised at what you see.'

- 'Here is the one action that makes the biggest difference.'

- 'This is the first time anyone has seen this data.'

2 **Tell them what to do**

In advance of showing the slide, *tell them what to do* once the slide is displayed.

Here are some choices:

- **Look at it**

  This is the simplest instruction:

  - 'Just take a look and we'll discuss it in a moment.'

  - 'Have a look and then I will go through it with you.'

  - 'Just familiarise yourself with the map, then I will explain where we will be going.'

- **Focus attention on an important part of the slide**

  This guides them:

  - 'I'd like you to look at the blue area because that's where the new office will be.'

  - 'Just focus on the red line in the graph.'

  - 'Look at the direction of the river.'

- **Engage their brain with a question**

  This gets them thinking:

  - 'I wonder if you can tell what the graph represents.'

  - 'See if you can identify which logo belongs to which company.'

  - 'Can you guess the missing percentage?'

TIP

Vary the type of introduction you use to keep things interesting.

---

3 **Show the slide**

Wait until *exactly* the right moment and then display the slide. Up until now, you have had their eye contact. The moment you show the slide they will look at the screen.

- **What if I can't remember which slide is coming next?**

  Solutions:

  - Print out a small version of the slides and keep it near you.

- Make a note in the notes section of your slide software if it has that facility.

● **Do I always have to introduce the slide first?**

No, there will be times when you can just show it and then speak, but, generally, you gain more by introducing it first.

Use the same three-step sequence for showing pre-prepared flipcharts.

Practise this sequence and it will soon be automatic.

Your turn

1 Choose a set of slides from one of your presentations.
2 For each slide, write a line about what you will say in advance of showing it.

Resource for further learning

Presentation Zen Design: A Simple Visual Approach to Presenting in Today's World (2013) by Garr Reynolds.

In-depth guidance on creating excellent slides and useful supplement to *Presentation Zen: Simple Ideas on Presentation Design and Delivery* by the same author.

Secret 53: How to keep the audience engaged when a slide is displayed

Once you have a slide displayed, you need to get the audience engaged so they focus on what is important. With certain exceptions, this means looking where you want them to look and guiding them with a gesture.

Why it matters

In the absence of such guidance, audience attention can be dispersed.

However, when you interact effectively with slides you:

- guide them to look *exactly* where you want them to look on the visual;
- maximise the chances of them getting the message you intend to convey;
- get full eye contact to land important points;
- keep control of the audience's attention throughout.

What to do

1 Stand in the best position

If you have a choice of where the screen goes, a good rule is to place it left of centre. Then position yourself in the centre, the most influential position, as shown in the picture below.

In TED talks speakers are usually in the centre – the most influential place to stand.

However, often the screen is in the centre as shown on the next page.

When the screen is in the centre, stand slightly to one side when showing slides as in the picture on the next page. Then, when not showing slides, move into the centre.

TIP

Do not stand too far to the side because you 'relegate' yourself to a less powerful position.

---

2   How to present a slide of bullet points

Let us assume you have introduced the slide before displaying it, as explained in the previous secret.

First:

- Look at it yourself as shown in the top picture opposite.

- The audience will automatically follow your eyes and look at it, too.

- Pause for a few seconds and let the audience absorb the information.

- Keep looking at the slide yourself.

People will look where you look.

Second:

- Gesture to the first bullet point as shown in the lower picture opposite.

- Refer to it while still looking at it: 'First, we have. . .'

- The audience will keep looking at it as you speak.

Third:

- Turn to look at the audience to elaborate as shown on the next page.

- The audience will move their gaze from the screen to look at you.

- This means you have their full eye contact.

You will land key messages with maximum impact when you look at the audience.

Once you have finished that point, repeat the same pattern again. 'Let's look at the second point', and so on. In this way, you stay in total control. It is an option to have the bullet points appear one by one. This is useful if you do not want people to see the whole list straight away.

3 How to present graphs and charts

When you first display the slide, the same applies as with bullet points. First, look at the data yourself and pause to let them look. Your next move depends on what you want to achieve.

If you want to talk about part of a graph and want them to be *focused on the relevant part* as you do so, you need to:

- gesture towards the relevant part; as in top picture opposite.

- start explaining it while *still looking* at it.

This will ensure they will keep looking at it.

- The moment you don't want the audience to look at the graph, turn back to them, for example, to make a point, or move onto something else as shown in the lower picture opposite.

- The audience will follow your eyes and turn their attention from the graph and back to you.

4 If you are presenting where the screen is behind you

For example, on a TED stage, where the speaker is normally in the centre and visuals are usually projected high and to the rear of the stage, do not:

- look at the screen;

- gesture towards it.

Doing so would cause you to keep turning around which would look odd.

Instead, the way to handle this is to:

- talk just like you would in the examples above;

- make it clear *from your words* when people need to look at the slide;

- make it *obvious with your voice tone* when you are making a key point and they will look back at you.

TIP

Press 'B' in PowerPoint to make the screen go black whenever you want.

Practise these skills when showing slides and they will soon become automatic.

Your turn

1 Choose slides from a presentation.

2 Practise *introducing* each slide using the three steps in Secret 52. Once a slide is displayed, *explain it* using the guidance above.

3 Ask for feedback, if possible.

Resource for further learning

Slide:ology: The Art and Science of Creating Great Presentations (2008) by Nancy Duarte.

Challenges traditional approaches to creating slides by teaching you to be a visual thinker.

8

How to ask and answer questions and finish

Secret 54: What happened when I asked them a question?

Presenting is not a one-way process. If you get the audience involved, you will get their engagement, too. Do this not just by *telling* but also *asking questions*.

Why it matters

Neuroscience shows that we can pay *conscious* attention to only one thing at a time. John Medina, author of *Brain Rules,* writes: 'Research shows that we can't multi-task.' A question hijacks the brain and grabs its attention. What this means is that, when you ask a question, you ensure the audience will focus on exactly what you want.

Eric Jensen, author of *Brain-Based Learning,* observes: 'Questions promote better learning.' He explains that: 'Asking questions also elicits deeper thinking than providing mere answers.' Well-chosen questions will strengthen people's understanding and recall of your talk.

Moreover, when you ask a question, it:

- turns the audience from passive to active mode;
- activates the meaning-seeking tendency of the brain;
- encourages people to think for themselves;
- promotes independent learning;

- increases ownership of the answers;

- demonstrates our belief in people to think of answers;

- increases the likelihood of people taking any actions mentioned in the question;

- persuades people more effectively than simply telling.

Mike noticed that the repeated enthusiasm of one audience member had started to annoy the others

Don't allow one person to dominate - involve others.

What to do

Ask questions that:

1 Reinforce learning

- 'What's the most important aspect of what you've just learnt?'

- 'How could you sum up the learning in a sentence?'

- 'What's the most surprising thing you have learnt?'

2 Help reflection

- 'Now how are you feeling about this?'

- 'Where are you now with this?'

- 'What's occurring to you as you think about this again?'

3 Apply learning

- 'What are three top tips to take away from today?'

- 'What's the most useful application for what you have learnt?'

- 'Where will you use what you have gained from today?'

4 Solve a problem

- 'What's causing this?'

- 'How can it be made to work?'

- 'What's the easiest way to get around this?'

5 Encourage creative ideas

- 'If there was a way to do it, what would it be?'

- 'Imagine you have already done it. How did you get there?'

- 'What would you do if you had a magic wand?'

6 Identify actions

- 'What's the one thing that would make the biggest difference?'

- 'What would be a quick win?'

- 'What's the next step?'

7 Imagine the positive future

- 'What would it be like next year if we did this?'

- 'What would be the effect on customers?'

- 'If everyone did this, what difference would it make?'

Try out the different types of questions and find out what works.

Your turn

For your next talk:

1 Choose at least three of the categories above and write questions for each.

2 Decide if you want people to answer aloud or in their head.

3 Decide where to incorporate the question in your talk.

Resource for further learning

The Art of Asking: Ask Better Questions, Get Better Answers (2008) by Terry J. Fadem.

See section on 'Types of Questions' for 25 types you can ask.

Secret 55: How to make sure the audience do not ask questions until you want them

Questions are signs that people are paying attention and curious. However, it can create problems if you have too many interruptions.

Why it matters

Problems with not knowing when questions will occur include:

● just knowing that people might interrupt can increase your nerves;

● interruptions can spoil your flow and train of thought;

● interruptions can make your presentation like a story that stops and starts;

- off-the-cuff questions can make it difficult to manage time;

- key messages may be diluted.

After all the interruptions at last week's briefing, Ruth took matters into her own hands

What to do

Let people know when you want questions.

TIP

People do not like being told what to do. However, if you ask with good reason, most will comply.

Use one of three main options:

1   Say you will take questions as you go along

It can sometimes be better to deal with questions as you go along, especially in small groups.

You might say:

'It makes sense to deal with questions as we go along. So if, at any time, you're not sure about anything, please ask. There will also be a chance at the end.'

2   Encourage them to ask questions at the end of sections

For some presentations, it may be unreasonable to make people wait until the very end. Let them know when ideally you would like questions.

You might say:

'I'll talk about each of the three project stages in turn. Unless it's a burning issue, I would ask you to hold questions until the end of each section because it will be time-efficient if we deal with them together.'

3   Reassure them there will be time for questions at the end

Especially with a large audience, it is more practical to take questions at the end.

You might say:

'If you think of anything as we go along, I'd ask you just to make a note because there will be a chance for questions at the end.'

With a smaller audience, you may decide not to be so absolute.

'Obviously, do shout if you think of something vital, but it works best if we can handle all questions together at the end.'

They still have a choice and most, if not all, will wait.

Further suggestions include:

● **Think ahead and anticipate questions and concerns**

If you have some idea of what questions might arise, you can flag them up early and reassure people that there will be a chance to discuss them later. This increases rapport and reduces the urge to jump in.

You might say:

'I am going to explain how the system works. However, I know that each of your departments is different. Therefore, once I have run through it, there will be a chance to raise any specific queries about your own situations.'

- **Mention question time in writing, such as on a slide or agenda paper**

  If there is a written agenda, you can include a time for questions. This will reinforce the request to hold questions until then.

Your turn

Think of a talk coming up and write down:

1 When you would like to take questions.

2 How you will let people know.

3 Phrases to encourage people not to ask questions before you want them.

Resource for further learning

The Presentation Coach: Bare Knuckle Brilliance for Every Presenter (2010) by Graham Davies.

Chapter 10 'Control the Day' has tips on getting things to go how *you* want, including when people ask questions.

Secret 56: Six ways to make question time collaborative

You might be dreading question time because you are not sure what people will ask, but there is a way to make it a positive experience. It is all about encouraging audience collaboration with you and with each other.

Why it matters

It matters because when it is not collaborative:

- a 'you versus them' session diminishes rapport;
- negativity reduces the strength of your message and can make a good talk end on a low point;

- your credibility can be threatened by aggressive questioning;

- you can feel defensive when under constant attack;

- your performance can suffer if you are 'on the back foot' too much.

On the other hand, there are great benefits of encouraging collaboration. People are far more inclined to put suggested changes into practice when they have discussed the issues. A collaborative question time, which includes discussion, can help to increase the chances of your audience taking action as a result of your talk.

Jenny had worried about questions, but having none felt worse

What to do

1   Set up the room to feel more collaborative

If you can choose the set-up, remember that some seating arrangements encourage collaboration more than others. Having people seated in groups at round tables café-style feels more collaborative than rows of seats theatre-style.

Even if you did not have any choice about room set-up, you may be able to make changes, such as asking people to arrange several chairs in a group to collaborate.

2 Frame the question session as collaborative

Introduce question time positively. Then the audience will view it through the lens of collaboration and will act accordingly.

Use phrases like:

- *'There's a lot of expertise in the room so, between us, I'm sure we can answer most queries.'* This clearly sets the frame that the audience will help answer questions.

- *'Now's the chance for us to discuss any issues you foresee.'* The word 'discuss' sets the frame of collaboration, rather than straight 'question and answer'.

- *'It will be great to have your ideas on how we can do this.'* This demonstrates that you value their input.

TIP

Use the word 'we' because it conveys the idea of working together.

---

3 Collect discussion questions on a flipchart during your talk

As questions arise, write those that require further discussion on a flipchart. Say that these will be discussed later. This reinforces your collaborative approach.

The key is to make it two-way – not just you answering questions.

4 Ask the audience for their help

People generally like to help because their contribution is valued. You can frame it as helping you: 'I have this idea and I'd appreciate your reactions to it.'

5 Use different ways to discuss a question

Research shows that the ideal number of people for a proper discussion is about seven to get everyone fully involved. However, even in large numbers, you can still have discussion elements by getting people working in smaller groups.

- Ask them to work in pairs. For example, ask them to spend two minutes discussing a question with the person seated next to them. Then select several pairs to share their answers.

- Set a question for them to discuss in small groups.

6   Draw on their experience

- Ask the whole group.

- Ask an expert.

- Ask a non-expert.

Encourage collaboration and make question time enjoyable and productive for all.

Your turn

Bring to mind the next talk you will do:

1   Write down three phrases you can say at the start of question time to encourage collaboration.

2   Make a note of three questions related to your talk that you could ask the group to help with. Choose the best to use first.

3   Write down ideas for discussion.

Resource for further learning

The Discussion Book: 50 Great Ways to Get People Talking (2016) by Stephen D. Brookfield and Stephen Preskill.

Ideas you can apply to presentations, meetings and classes and many more situations.

Secret 57: Do not end your talk immediately after question time

When there are no more questions, speakers will sometimes say: 'Any more questions? No? . . . Thank you very much.' On the face of it, this sounds fine.

However, what you really need to do is say something more because, otherwise, it can reduce the chances of people acting on your call-to-action.

Why it matters

If question time was difficult for you:

- you end on a low and that can deflate your argument;
- those difficulties will stay in their minds – people remember what happens *last*;
- your core message might be lost;
- people may leave with negative energy, which will not help your cause.

However, if you *say something* after question time, then you can:

- reframe a difficult question time into a positive;
- lift the mood;
- reinforce your core message and your call-to-action;
- paint a positive mental picture of the future.

Terry always liked to end on a high after a difficult 'Question Time'

What to do

1 Put question time just before the end of your talk

Leave time to say something more after question time. Even a minute or two may suffice.

After the last question, follow this sequence:

- Summarise your key message.

- Make your 'call-to-action'.

- Describe the 'new reality' by saying what will happen as a result of their actions.

See more detail on how to do these three steps in Secret 60.

2 If question time has to be at the end – still say something after it

If you speak at a conference, often it is arranged so that speakers take questions at the very *end* of their talk. In this instance, *still say something after the questions.* Even a few words will be enough to create a positive ending.

You will have already given a *key message summary, call-to-action* and *explained the difference it will make* as part of your talk. Therefore, to repeat that in detail is not appropriate. Instead, give a *brief version of the same sequence*:

- 'Thank you for your questions.'

- 'So, the key thing to remember is x (insert your key message).'

- 'Therefore, once again, I'd urge you to . . . (insert call-to-action).'

- 'Then, as a result, we can all look forward to . . . (insert the difference their actions will make).'

TIP

Practise the above sequence until it is automatic and you will always end on a high.

---

3 End question time when you are 'on the up'

Anything you can do to end question time on a positive note is helpful. If you feel question time is nearly finished, and there is a good feeling in the room, then you could end it there. Go on to make your closing remarks.

4 After a difficult question time, transition to a positive

Beware of trying to lift the mood too suddenly. If people are in a negative frame of mind, they will not instantly flip into a positive one.

The secret is to '*pace*' and '*lead*' the audience from the negative feeling to the positive. See Secret 12 for more on pacing and leading.

Here is an example:

● 'Thank you for your questions on those difficult issues.'

● 'As we can see, this is a not an easy process.'

● 'However, the key point I'd like you to take away is x.'

● 'I again ask you to join me in . . . (insert your call-to-action).'

● 'With your support, I am sure we will be able to . . . (insert what the positive outcome will be).'

● 'Thank you.'

Always end on a high to increase the chance of your audience taking action.

Your turn

1 For your next talk, write down key points you will say after question time.

2 Memorise the closing couple of lines.

3 Practise on a colleague and ask for feedback.

Resource for further learning

Resonate: Present Visual Stories that Transform Audiences (2010) by Nancy Duarte.

Chapter 2 has sample 'calls-to-action' and helpful tips on ending.

Secret 58: How to manage question time

Question time can be difficult to manage. However, this eight-step sequence will help you to handle it professionally and maximise its value to everyone.

Why it matters

- A poorly handled session can reflect badly on you.

- People can get frustrated if their questions are not addressed.

- A successful session can boost your credibility.

- Handling questions well can strengthen the impact of your talk.

The staff mood confirmed that five minutes for questions wasn't enough

What to do

Follow these eight steps for managing question time.

1 Introduce the question session

You might include:

- setting a positive tone by saying you welcome questions, comments and ideas;
- managing expectations: 'We have ten minutes for questions.'

See Secret 56 for help on making question time collaborative.

2 Ask encouragingly

- Instead of: 'Do you have any questions?' ask: 'What questions do you have?'
- Open your arms to be encouraging.
- Do not put your hands behind your back.
- Do not step back – it may appear that you are retreating.

3 Connect and listen

- When hands go up, choose one person.
- Connect with the open palm gesture towards them and make eye contact.
- Say their name, if you know it: 'Yes, Mary.' If you do not know their name, then ask them.
- Give your full attention while they ask their question.
- Avoid saying, 'Great question' because they may feel you are judging or condescending.
- Repeat the question if people cannot hear it.

4 Answer their question

If their input is not a question but an objection, see Secret 59. Otherwise:

- Answer concisely.
- If you do not know the answer, say so.
- Give a reason why you do not know or cannot say.

- Consider asking if an audience member knows, in which case, *redirect the question* to them. Alert them *first* by using their name: 'John, you've had a lot of experience with that project, what light can you shed on this?'

- Or you might *rebound the question* to the questioner: 'It looks like that's important to you Michael. What are your own thoughts?'

- Or open the question up to the audience. This is called an '*overhead question*' because you 'throw' it over the heads of the audience.

- If the question still cannot be answered, say you will find out for them.

TIP

For a question outside the scope of your talk, or of no interest to the audience, say you will help the person afterwards.

---

5 Keep everyone involved by making eye contact as you answer

If the answer is brief, just look at the questioner.

If the answer is longer, involve the audience as follows:

- Start by looking at the questioner.

- Then look at some of the others.

- Return your attention to the questioner.

- Repeat this alternating pattern.

- Give about a third of eye contact time to the questioner and the remainder to the others.

6 Check that you have answered their question

'Does that answer your question?'

- If 'No', ask what more help they need.

- If 'Yes', thank them for their question and move to step 7.

7 Open up for more questions

Ask: 'Any more questions?' and start steps 2 to 6 again.

8   Close the question session

Thank them for their questions and move on to your final words. See Secret 60 for help on how to deliver a powerful ending.

What if two people are speaking at once?

- Hold an arm towards one of them and make the *'stop'* gesture used by police to halt traffic. This universal stop sign will cause most people to stop talking.

- Say you will let them speak in a moment.

Use the eight steps each time and you will get used to controlling question time.

Your turn

1   Next time someone asks you questions in conversation, practise giving concise answers.

2   For your next talk, write down questions you might be asked and plan your answers.

3   Ask someone to pose those questions to you and practise answering. Then ask for feedback.

Resource for further learning

The Presentation Coach: Bare Knuckle Brilliance for Every Presenter (2010) by Graham Davies.

Chapter 11 'Control Q & A', has plenty of practical tips for handling questions.

Secret 59: Handle objections by being curious

No matter how well you plan a talk, you may still receive objections such as: 'I can't see that working,' 'That's all very well, but. . . ' or 'I'm not convinced.' Therefore, being able to respond is vital and when you handle an objection well it becomes a positive.

Why it matters

The way you handle objections affects your impact:

- If you struggle, it can reduce your credibility.

- A good response shows you have thought things through.

- Strong answers strengthen your argument.

- You increase trust when you respond well.

- Knowledgeable answers demonstrate authority in your field.

Lynn's method for handling objections unfortunately relied on audience cooperation

What to do

If there is an obvious answer, then give it.

As in the objections above, people often generalise and give limited information.

In these instances, beware of jumping to an immediate defence because:

- almost certainly, you do not have enough information from the audience member to give a good answer;

- they may feel that you are dismissing their point;
- it may lead to a 'ping-pong' effect as you argue the case.

Instead, follow these six steps:

1 Encourage

Avoid being defensive and instead be *curious*.

- Keep body language open.
- Do not fold your arms.
- Remember not to step back as if retreating.

2 Ask a question

- Gives you thinking time.
- Gains information.
- Well-phrased questions can politely challenge generalisations.

The choices are:

● Closed questions

'Is that true?'

Requires a *'yes'* or *'no'* answer.

● Limiting questions

'Are you concerned about the people, processes or the product?'

Limits the answers.

● Open questions

'What is the main problem?'

'What' and *'how'* questions yield additional information.

Two directions for questions:

● Explore the problem

'What makes you say that?'

'Can you say more?'

'How often does that happen?'

- **Move towards a solution**

    'How do you think we could get around this?'

    'What would help?'

    'What would make the biggest difference?'

> TIP
>
> Do not ask 'why?' or 'why not?' questions in response to their objection.

'Why do you say that?' can make things worse by:

- putting the audience member on the back foot;
- making them feel they have to justify themselves;
- creating a 'you versus them' feeling, like being interrogated.

Don't repeat negative or hostile words.

In response to: 'That's a terrible idea' do not repeat 'terrible' in your answer because it highlights the negative word.

Use the person's name because it helps rapport.

3 Demonstrate listening

As they reply, do not *just* listen – instead, *make it obvious* that you are listening:

- Make eye contact.
- Use nods.
- Give your *full* attention.

4 Summarise

Summarise their response and check your understanding:

- It shows you have listened.
- If you listen to them, they are more likely to listen to you.
- It shows common understanding.

Useful phrases:

- 'Have I understood you correctly?'
- 'Is that your point?'
- 'Have I summarised your point accurately?'

If they say 'no' – return to step 2.

If they say 'yes' – continue to step 5.

5 Respond

Respond with one of the following:

- provide an answer;
- ask for their thoughts;
- ask the audience.

6 Check

Check you have answered to their satisfaction.

- 'Does that answer your question?'
- 'Is that OK?'
- 'Does that explain it for you?'

If they say 'yes', thank them.

If they say 'no' or 'not quite', then you might ask:

- 'What are you still not sure about?'
- 'How can I help?'
- 'Which part have I not fully explained?'

What if I cannot answer their concern?

- If you do not know, say so.
- Give a reason why you do not know.
- Say you will get back to them.

As you get used to handling objections, you will soon feel more comfortable.

Your turn

1   Next time someone challenges you in conversation, instead of defending yourself, try asking them an open question.

2   Practise the six steps with someone before your next talk.

3   Ask someone to practise the six steps *on you* so you know what it feels like.

Resource for further learning

NLP at Work:– The Difference that Makes a Difference in Business (2002) by Sue Knight.

Chapter 6 'Precision Questions' is very useful to develop questioning skills that will help you to handle numerous challenging situations. The book is excellent support for communication skills and numerous other applications of NLP.

Secret 60: End on a high, not a whimper

The way you end your talk is critical if it is to have its desired effect. Yet so many talks end in ways that are less than uplifting. Phrases like: 'Well, that's all we've got time for, so thank you,' are all too common. However, a well thought-out ending can inspire your audience and ignite their passion to do something because of your talk.

Why it matters

There are numerous reasons to end well:

● It is a chance to reinforce your message.

● The audience remember what you say last.

● They are left with a positive impression of you.

● A great ending can inspire your audience.

- Uplifting endings can motivate people to take action.

- It can improve your confidence for future presentations.

Doreen always tried to end on a high, but the team's euphoric reaction took even her by surprise

What to do

Help them see the big picture of a positive future.

Do three things to end on a high:

1 Make sure they have got your key message

You could:

- summarise your key points;

- repeat your key message;

- have your key message on the screen;

- show a powerful visual that says it all;

- use a quote that encapsulates your message.

2 Ask for your 'call-to-action'

This is where you get the audience thinking about applying what you have spoken about.

What do you want them to do?

Phrasing examples

- 'So, what about your situation? Where is this useful for you?'

- 'I'd like you to spread this important message.'

- 'So, next time you encounter this kind of experience, what will you do differently?'

When you include questions in your call-to-action, it helps people think for themselves.

TIP

Make your call-to-action an easy step to increase the likelihood that people will take it.

---

3 Describe the new reality: how will things be different?

- Bring to life what things will be like as a result of the call-to-action.

- Paint a picture of how things will be different. This moves people into that future in their minds. Imagining a positive can inspire people to support you.

Chris Anderson, Head of TED, describes this as 'camera pull-back' and explains it thus:

At the end, why not show us the bigger picture, a broader set of possibilities implied by your work.

To make this ending as powerful as possible, you need to describe just how wide and far-reaching the benefits of taking the action could be. Explain how their actions can have a 'domino effect' as one action causes another.

- Talk about benefits in the short, medium or long term.
- Highlight benefits for as many people or situations as possible, such as individuals, teams, customers, clients or patients.

For example:

- 'By next week we will start to see improvements.'
- 'Just imagine this time next year . . . how different it could all be.'
- 'Think what a difference we can all make.'

Use the energy of your voice and body language to inject enthusiasm into you words. Once you have delivered your final line, just say 'thank you'. This will prompt a round of applause from the audience.

Make it obvious to the audience that you have ended.

Otherwise, it is like a musical performance where people start clapping because they thought it was the end. Or did not clap because they thought the performance had not finished.

TIP

Write a powerful final line – and practise saying it so it sounds like your final line.

Your turn

1 Think of a talk you have coming up.
2 Write key phrases for your ending, based on the three points above.

Resource for further learning

'Can we create new senses for humans?' by David Eagleman, TED2015 (20-minute video).

Example of how to build a powerful ending over the final few minutes.

Observing presentations – what to look for

Content and structure

- Strong introduction – grabbing attention and making the audience care.
- Clear key message(s) – made obvious and easy to remember.
- Logical flow – easy to follow.
- Contrast – varied pace and rhythm, keep the interest of the audience.
- Phrasing – using words that bring ideas to life.
- Appeal to head and heart.
- Stories – to make it memorable and create emotion.
- Metaphors – to make ideas easy to absorb: 'It's like . . . '
- Case studies – and relevant examples and suitable evidence,
- Startling facts – surprising facts and surprising statistics.
- Strong ending summary – highlight key message, call-to-action and the difference it will make.

Visuals

- Slides are varied, e.g. include memorable pictures, graphs, diagrams.
- Effectiveness of other visuals, such as flipchart or whiteboard.
- Well introduced and explained.

Presentation style

- Energy – presenter shows enthusiasm and believes in what they are saying.
- Voice – well projected, varied in speed, pitch and volume to create interest.
- Eye contact – is maintained with audience.
- Gestures – strong descriptive gestures along with gestures for emphasis.
- Stance – a confident stance enhancing the credibility of the presenter.

Be specific in your feedback: give examples of what you see and hear along with the positive or negative effects.

Observer's feedback form

Presenter _____

Observer _____

Talk, speech or presentation title _____

1 What works well

2 What to do differently next time

Thank you for your comments

Index